FarmKid

Tales of growing up in rural America

Justin Isherwood

Badger Books Inc.
Oregon, Wis.

Badger Books Inc./Waubesa Press
P.O. Box 192
Oregon, WI 53575
Toll-free phone: (800) 928-2372
Fax: (608) 835-3638
Email: books@badgerbooks.com
Web site: www.badgerbooks.com

Library of Congress Cataloging-in-Publication Data

Isherwood, Justin.
    Farm kid : tales of growing up in rural America / Justin Isherwood.
        p. cm.
    ISBN-13: 978-1-932542-15-8
    ISBN-10: 1-932542-15-9
    1. Isherwood, Justin--Childhood and youth. 2. Isherwood, Justin--Homes and haunts--Wisconsin. 3. Authors, American--20th century--Biography. 4. Wisconson--Social life and customs. 5. Farmers--Wisconsin--Biography. 6. Rural families--Wisconsin. 7. Farm life--Wisconsin. 8. Children--Wisconsin. I. Title.

    PS3559.S435Z466 2005
    813'.54--dc22

                                                        2005008201

To farmland and those who tend it.
May they endure

Contents

Farmkid

I, it says the center of every soul, am a farmkid. Not pilot, not banker, not lumberjack, not nurse or flight attendant, not mother, not father, not priest, not philosopher or physicist … but … a farmkid. A farmkid be the soul.

I was born to what pastures a soul must have, an open sort of place. I had chicken pox when I was seven, maybe it was eight, had mumps and pinkeye and assorted stuff. I had a dog, a tree house, I raised chickens for 4-H, and ate 'em.

I ran away from home regularly but came back for the sake of fresh bread. I collected leaves and thought I was wealthy, collected stones and thought it bullion; sticks, gopher skulls, bird eggs, cobwebs that were so delicate. And a hundred other things that didn't fit in a box or under the bed.

I watched stuff die, it was mean and awful and very cruel. We ate 'em for supper so it wasn't so bad. Uncle Fred was eaten too, by a silo filler as chewed him up and swallowed the lot. I remember they closed the lid of his box. It wasn't so bad.

There was a fox earth at the end of the home pasture where I chased cows. I put my finger in cow poop. Once. Twice, at least twice. I don't know why, I didn't die.

A lady older than sin lived in the house down the road, she had a blue jay for a friend and died one winter week before she was found, sad, the paper said. Wasn't so bad.

I lived in a house bigger than a hill, slept on summer nights under the porch, built a shack, learned to weld, milk cows, fill the silo, bale hay, pick potatoes, cut wood, a hundred other jobs and still not half done.

I had a crow for a pet, a raccoon, badger, skunk, ducks, cats, chickens, cows, pigeons. They were my friends if not my brother and sister. Ate 'em. It wasn't so bad.

I was born to English stock, maybe it was Polish with some hint of Irish. Coulda been Norwegian if someone remembered, Finland even, some far before place. The other half of me was Indian, Arapaho and musk ox. The census doesn't report my prairie birth. Same as Sitting Bull I had mud in my veins and acorns for organs.

I was a red man on the inside, through and through, Boy Scout, too. I tramped the woods, went to school, sang in the choir, attended church. Still, it didn't wash off, the thing inside, as made me wonder what other folks were.

I was born a farmkid, you can tell by the scars; that one was barbed wire. Didn't the stove leave a nice design? I'm marked by the way I walk and the way I stop to look at things others can't see. I'm terrible in traffic, always looking for something on the other side of the fence.

I like night a lot better than a modern person should. To go with darkness is the creature in me. I am owl and raccoon, brown bat and fox. I can smell things others can't, you learn this skill early. I smell hay and motors. I smell pine and maple, potato blight and bad teeth. I can smell a clutch slipping, the cow in heat, fire in the woods. Fear too is quite volatile and you can smell the difference between it and too much perfume.

I like things others think are groady, I like my hands dirty, I like to be hungry and sweat hard and breathe hard, too. As is way too weird for most places I've been.

The farmkid soul is a hard thing to shake. I've seen people try, then when they are alone you find them talking to a tree. Farmkid for sure.

Hay Legs

Hay legs is the same as sea legs except hay legs is dry land. Sea legs is what a person gets on a big puddle of water, or else ends up puking their innards overboard for longer than is pleasurable. The inference being those who don't acquire sea legs are as good as stitched in the shroud, a disagreeable way to get your money's worth out of a cruise.

Hay legs has to do with haying. Haying one of the more negative attributes of agriculture, conducted like as not on the hottest, humidest, most breathless days of summer. In the Hellenic Age of hay, as so happened to coincide with my childhood, baling hay is what we did every waking moment from the day school let out until it reassembled. The only punctuation of this was potato vacation. Then corn picking vacation, followed by stove-wood vacation, then seed-cutting vacation, whereafter the whole business started over. After haying all summer we looked forward to the vacations, even if they were potatoes and stovewood.

The bulk of my childhood I realize now was devoted to the consummate comfort of a milk cow's internal organs.. Either I was in the business of actively shoveling something into the beast or else shoveling something out. I might as well have been a coal stoker on a dreadnought, such was this animal's capacity for ingress and egress. If tourists visiting Cape Canaveral are impressed by the enormous fuel tank used to supply the main engines of the Space Shuttle, they ought to see the supply required to keep a cow whose cud is the one perpetual motion device known to exist in the universe. The most unceasing animal ever to eat on the planet earth. As luck did have it, my fate was to provide sustenance for this unquenchable creature.

Happily, I was born to a mechanical age, when but a generation previous tending a cow was done by hay fork and horse-drawn. At least my age was served by a device known to its inmates as a hay baler. In reality, the baler was a combination of several mechanical principles; namely the battering ram from the Middle Ages, the Archimedian screw courtesy of the Greeks, the French guillotine, and finally the Norwegian single-seat outhouse. These superior devices when combined by forces of evolution did create the self-tie, automatic eject, continuous feed, bite-size, cutely dimensioned hay baler. Using this instrument, a field of hay was rendered into a neat three-dimensional package that in turn could be carried, piled, carried some more, repiled but higher this time. During the summer 90 percent of our waking hours were seemingly devoted to carrying hay bales from one place to another. All this corresponding devotion in effort to stay in front of that unquenchable cow. If kids in other places feared the Bengal tiger, feared the wolf, the grizzly bear who in an awful moment might eat them, we feared instead the ruthless milk cow. Forever eating. Explaining why we were forever haying.

Unfortunately to the business of hay, badgers lived in this same countryside as did dwell the hay wagon and the unappeasable cow. The badger as you will rightly recall is the animal that invented golf in the kingdom of the ancient Chippewa, who didn't quite pick up on the game despite the game as perfected by the badger was superior in all respects to that contest credited to the Scots. The aboriginal contest being a mix between whole-body basketball, pinball and interment. A sport as would have been spectacular on television had the tribe that invented the game survived the prototype.

Badger golf, as might be guessed, is a precipitous affair, because a badger hole is some bit bigger than a standard golf hole. Played well, I mean badger hole golf, tourists and untrainable children vanish without a trace. Some believe this is a good thing. It happened the region of my youth was by purest coincidence the very best badger real estate anywhere in the world. The difference was in a word ... sand. Perfect, unblemished, extra virgin, make that double extra virgin sand, where even an arthritic old badger can dig away to their heart's content and never once strike an impediment worse than sling-shot gravel. So happy were badgers in this dominion that they dug burrows for pleasure. Just the pleasure of digging. The joy of digging. The spiritual delight of digging. Badger civilization instead of ski chalets, deer shacks and lakeside cottages had burrows. Hundreds, thousands of burrows. Some became collectors of burrows, antique burrows, preserving them in their original and getting them listed on the national registry of historic burrows. The result was every hayfield became honeycombed with badger holes, a few of which were national treasures. The effect of these burrows on a hay wagon is the same as gale force eight off the coast of Cape Horn. A common wagon becomes instead the pitching terrible deck of a square rigger caught in the furies. An unhardened person set on a hay wagon soon had both legs broken from the wagon dropping out from beneath their feet, only to rebound an instant later while the victim's legs were yet at full extension. Wondering, like is natural, where the wagon deck had disappeared to. This only being the standard symmetrical hay wagon badger hole drop as opposed to the asymmetrical drop where one side of the wagon is descending while the other ascending, and even the experienced hay wagon walker can be maimed.

The secret of hay legs was to assume the oft ridiculed stance of the professional seafarer, this bowlegged pose acts like a natural shock absorber. Allowing the wagon to disappear from beneath the person, yet he not entirely losing contact with the deck. A quality hayrack rider kept their knees bent at an angle to average out the travel of the hayrack between full free fall and full perihelion. It looked ridiculous to passersby, and they laughed at us. Calling us hayseeds and other such aphorisms. In the next instant their front wheel hitting a badger hole and everybody inside the car had switch teeth and undergarments. Such is a seismic nature of an average quality badger hole.

When Elvis Presley shocked the moral standards of the world forty years ago, his stage gryations were believed by most critics to be of a sexual theme. Despite it was obvious to every kid native to the hay wagon hay that Elvis had at some time been employed likewise and learned rock and roll from the original.

Regular Meeting of the Howzitso

The regular weekly meeting of the Howzitso Society began with a pledge of allegiance. A variable oath, one week our faith was in bicycles, the next to BB guns, another to the Milwaukee Braves, snapping turtles and an older brother's *Sun and Health* magazine. What was sacred and important to us varied with the season, and the number of days in a row we had been shackled to the hay wagon, or the stone boat, or the potato field. Sometimes it didn't take very much to be sacred, as long as it was somewhere else than the potato grading shed.

Holy objects, we realized, had the habit of being useless, which is why they were deemed holy in the first place. Holy consisted of those things as did not change, which just sat there, or were perfectly useless whether they moved or not. Math was holy 'cause math just sat there. It was an honor code among Howzitso members to hate math and none was allowed to get any better grade in math than a C minus. It would mean showing affection to something of not very high intelligence. Math hadn't changed in four million years, same old frustrating jumble of functions, math was dumber than a dead pine snake. Meaning we had lots of affection for pine snakes when they was alive and stealthful in the marsh grass or hanging out among the willow trees down by the creek. A pine snake could scare the bicuspids out of the back door of a kid owing a pine snake has the almost exact same pattern as a diamond-back rattler. A pine snake is a perfectly nice snake and is only deadly by association. Deadlier than a spitting cobra, more deadly than a pitiless slit-eyed viper or nasty-minded bushmaster. Those snakes killed with poisons which is bad enough, a pine snake killed by facsimile. It scared a kid to death because it resembled toxic substance. Merely seeing a pine snake was enough to kill a kid. Your heart raced so fast it burst the blood vessels and tore a person to smithereens, the kid as dead and splattered as if struck head-on by a twelve-ton meteorite.

The Howzitso Club was sometimes a club, sometimes a society, didn't make any difference though society sounded more refined. When exactly was our weekly meeting depended on when we could get loose from farm chores. For farmkids this is a major obstacle and it meant sometimes we just had to plain vanish. Mama called it evaporation. "Where'd you kids evaporate to?" she'd say. I don't ever recall saying where it was we went, thinking if she believed in our evaporation we ought just leave it as that. There is nothing more obvious to a farm child than the farm was the worst sort of occupation it is possible to load on an adult animal, made all the worse when the left-overs are applied to the offspring. I remember thinking if a person wants to be a farmer that is their own business, but what right did they have to drag innocent children to that same purgatory? Farmers should all be celibate, I thought, same as nuns and priests, so they can worship on their own dime.

Weren't ever a moment, a minute, not a nanosecond free from farm chores. Correspondingly, we hated chores.

It was one thing to look agricultural, to see a barn or field; it was another to crawl after it with a pitchfork, hoe handle and shovel. Mr. Lincoln in his Emancipation Proclamation forgot to mention farmkids of white and freckled races. The result being if we were ever to be free of bondage and oppression we were obligated to free ourselves. This then was our counterinsurgence, that we accomplished under the pretext of actually doing chores. Our ally in this was the farm itself, and using the farm size to our advantage; oppression loses something when it exceeds 80 acres. At 300 acres a kid can gain something resembling a judicial review, meaning we looked well enough like we were headed for chores. But somewhere out of sight of the house we switched tracks and what was supposed to be an afternoon fixing fence was instead an afternoon down by the creek and another oath-bound secret cabal of the Howzitso.

A meeting of the Howzitso never met without kindling the secret altar, the fire-de-camp; unless it was just too blame hot for fire. The fire was a basic tenet of farmkids, and it was likewise for the Howzitso. We liked fire, we adored fire, we worshipped fire. Every time we met we had a fire unless it was likely to give the meeting away, meaning someone was like to know we weren't fixin' fence. The particulars of a fire didn't matter as long as it was fire. We did not know why we so liked fire but we did and fire mesmerized us and we could stare into the beatitude of fire for hours and drift and talk and drift some more and see things in fire we didn't know we knew until sitting by a fire, which is why fire is hallowed. At least hallowed to the Howzitso.

Every Howzitso member carried two required ritual objects, a jackknife and a kitchen match. It was with these two elements a farmkid knew he or she could build anything, survive anything, endure anything ...

build a gingerbread house in the wilds of Kansas using sod only, or survive the winter on the Arctic ice pack. To be found without the obligatory kit of the Howzitso was grounds for immediate suspension. A match could save a kid's life, Jack London said as much. A match is the difference between life and death, hot and cold, wet and dry, raw and otherwise. This was the reason for our rigorous training with matches. Every member of us could kindle a fire at the drop of a hat, or if need be in a hat. Kindle a bonfire in the middle of a monsoon with no more than fresh seaweed and beach sand. The matches were the Howzitso's own special-issue; paraffin-coated, foul-wrapped, varnished and shellacked, impervious to weather, moisture and the Dow Jones. Any member who did not have on their person a match of the Howzitso was liable to excommunication. The standard test was to pee on the match; if it still lit, your membership in the Howzitso remained valid.

Our treasury consisted of a White Owl cigar box filled with various kinds and conditions of jackknives; knives we had found, traded or were deemed by others beyond repair. We retained in this box all the wounded, lost, fabulous, old, ancient, antique, junk pile that we ever came across; paring knives, butcher knives, toe stabbers, daggers, swords, skein dhus, dirks, claymores, switchblades, brass-walled jackknives as had lost their genuine bone handles. The bone not being as genuine as supposed. Every old knife we could find was given a haven of rest and respect.

If atomic war ever happened, we were prepared. Our treasury of necessary things was stashed in the hollow butternut about midway in the woods between Bannock's dam and the first bridge crossing over to the Buena Vista Marsh. Also known as Whittaker's bridge owing that the hand of Armatous Whittaker was seen here. This where folks throw tobacco money being Armatous was a saint of agriculture on account he was the first person to explore the innards of an Allis Chalmers silage chopper. The onlyest piece of him to survive intact was his hand, the rest of him high moisture protein mixed with some nice corn silage. A saint 'cause Armatous died, 'cause he didn't shut off the PTO, didn't quench the hurry in him, thought he was faster than the machine, thought supper would get cold. As a result, saint Armatous saved other farmers from doing the same. As explained why he was a saint if only a local saint, and why we pitched what was left of him a penny every time we cross the Whittaker bridge.

We liked matches. Not only because matches caused fire but for the match itself. Few things besides sex, which we understood theoretically, was as amazing and deserving of reverence as a match. Imagine, a mere stick of wood, a mineralized head, combined with a striking surface and in that interlude an inarticulate twig becomes fire. Nuclear fusion appeared no more wonderful to us than a common match. Slid down the barrel of a BB gun a match became an entertainment. On dark nights we spent hours shooting match heads at the old stone bridge, enthralled how they struck and spent their phosphors, trailing behind a cometary banner. This was a great thing to do on a blacktop road on an equally dark night. The matches skipping ahead like tracer bullets. In the green night of July we didn't fear setting fire to anything since it was too humid to burn anything.

To fire were we devoted. Fire we reasoned was the first religion, we knew this in our bones. The Howzitso sat by fires of all sorts: campfires and leaf smogs, incendiaries of tinderous Christmas trees, smoldering garbage heaps. The fire conjoined us, the fire held our most earnest rapture. We met around sticks and twigs, a fuming pile of sawdust that sparkled and fussed, leaf fires that coughed and ruminated. We hunked around all fires; bark fires as stink, we burned straw, we burned manure, we burned bones and shingles, we burned *Life* magazines, they smoked terrible. Hay burned with an aromatic glint, the very air was given a perfume and tonic. We burned these and all other things. Anything for a fire, a fire to stare at and say our deep secrets to. Our coven met by eventide and nightfall bearing with us boards and laths and any else thing, sawmill slabs and old doors, window putty and catalogs that burned forever if soaked in fuel oil. Around these kindles we spent lifetimes. We burned bones and cowskulls and watched tormented fire rise in the eye sockets, fiery thoughts in cow brains, we never knew before how deeply cows thought.

Of the fire we asked both the unholy query and the plain. How come the world is? How come man is supreme? How is it so that in a hundred million years the puniest, spindle-legged thing owns the majority of Creation? Unless ... The club specialized in unless. Unless it only seems so because we are looking now and now is soon dispatched. What if human beings are only uncooked fossils, undone and soon enough extinct as everything else? Wouldn't that be heck, we thought, and then unthought it. The more we thought the more obvious it became. We felt good about the world again, knowing exactly where we were and how it was gonna end and was good because the game wasn't cheated and knowing God wouldn't cheat. We went on to harder questions. How's it so that light goes a hundred, hundred, thousand million billion miles and still ain't slower than it was when it started? Does the universe run downhill? What if the universe really is forever out there and goes and goes and goes and doesn't ever stop except for wide places in the dark? What if there are islands of universes and more islands and then even more islands? In the dark of a farm night it is an amazingly good sensation to feel so insignificant. How's it so that geese know when to come and where to go? And how do swallows know how to return to the barn eaves? How's it so a cow with a skull the size of a chest of drawers is dumber than a teapot? How's it so you always think the scariest things when you're alone? How's it so...

The Howzitso ended when our neighbor Tom Soik moved to the village. It ended when I fell in love with a girl. It ended when my brother Gary went to law school. Though every time I sit by a fire I realize once you belong to Howzitso, you always belong.

Immortality and Cats

The world once had, as every farmkid believed, an inexhaustible supply of cats, the same was true of chickens. Cats reproduced like flies, grandfather said. I tried for awhile to imagine cats doing sordid things in midair. I couldn't. From then on I believed cats reproduced like angels. The correct answer is angels don't reproduce, least not how you think, but instead come out of nowhere, the reconstituted vapors of deceased Christians. The same way Ma made orange juice out of powder from a can and water, which was as close to nowhere as I could then imagine. Cats, I once thought, were like concrete. The essence of cat was a concentrated powder that when poured from a bag was mixed with whatever local leftovers. Cats were exotic sorts of animals so they probably started out as some exotic leftovers, most likely Hindus or Chinamen who on their death evaporate and when they hit the next dew-point emerged as cats. Farm children end up with some pretty strange theories of how things came to be, but since the practice is private no damage is done.

The farm, where I myself commenced from equally obscure beginnings, had cats. I would say billions of cats but you'd think me a liar. To satisfy the reader as to the truth of my remarks, I will say there were only millions of cats, knowing I'm underestimating their presence just so you'll believe it. Thousands didn't come near to numbering those cats. Should an impartial observer set up on any midsummer afternoon on the ridge row of the barn... meaning the barn whose crow-nest window faced east and with a bit of agility and some luck reach across to the lightning rod cable and hoisted their carcass over the end boards onto the roof... as demonstrates the problem of being an impartial observer in the first place. The perspective, like as not, is not an easy place to get to in the first place. Meaning the barn roof. Still if it's the spectacle of cats you want to witness, this was the place to establish impartiality.

Midsummer was the finest spectacle of cats a person can hope to see, there are cats at every corner of the farm. Cats spread out in an undiluted layer, as far as the eye can see, cats. Any mathematician will tell that multiplying the number of acres by the number of cats per acre yields the approximate number of cats on any one farm. A glance at the clover field demonstrated that for every six linear feet of clover there is at least one cat and probably an apprentice. That makes 220 cats per quarter section per six foot swath. So the actual number of cats was 220 squared or forty-four thousand and some extra to carry luggage. This might or might not include the apprentices, hangers on and those who traveled some distance to attend a funeral. Our farm consisted of 314 acres, all of it overrun with cats which if you've been keeping track is 8.2 million cats not including those visiting relatives or those too sick to work.

It was a natural offshoot of this abundance of cats that they should become the experimental medium of farmboys. Particularly those of Methodist extraction who wished to conduct theological research on lower animals before trying any of several pulpit cures on their own persons. So it was we tested immortality with cats. In this test we provided Sunday School classes for underage cats, in order to determine whether they went on to more productive and God-fearing lives, because they were exposed to early lessons in which good people knew who they were in the first place, and bad people was anybody else. Nothing seemed to indicate that cats were improved by Sunday School. On other cats we forced bad habits. We deprived these cats of spinach, forced them to go without oatmeal, meatloaf, mashed potatoes. Very soon it was apparent these cats did not go into hard-core delinquency or hang out at pool halls. At the time, we did not know what we proved other than to know similar experiments ought not be performed on unetherized patients, not to mention, farmkids.

My childhood was consumed with space flight, every kid wanted to be an astronaut, and during haying season would have volunteered to go into space, with or without the space suit. We reasoned it couldn't be that much worse than the haymow. When it came to space flight and the attendant problems of reentry we experimented with cats, requesting volunteers. Cats, like farmkids, were always willing. While it cost millions to perfect the Atlas-Mercury program at Cape Canaveral, we did the same research at far less cost from the top of the silo. One tin can, one lid, preferably a screw top, and one cat and you were ready to test three basic elements of space travel: free fall, gravity and the sudden stop. We wrote the cats name and serial number on the silo if the chute didn't open.

The cat sometimes protested and had to be cajoled into entering the tin can; we told the cat that the whole business was insured and that it was a better quality tin can. If the cat persisted in its protest we employed the selective service draft and just jammed the cat into the can, turned on the lid and launched it off the silo. To be a full and competent test, the can had to undergo a series of retro-maneuvers at which the cat set up a sustained yeowling that in turn allowed you to track the vehicle to the ground, at which point the yeowling stopped.

The reader might have at this point an inclination to feel remorse for the cat; there is no need. We gave all the volunteers a written guarantee of the final resurrection and that they would be allowed to become angel cats without the bother of paying pew rent or the requirement to have a minister at the funeral. Which was a lot better deal than that given to Christians, besides these cats were former Hindus and at 8,200,000 per farm not including chattels, minor children and mothers-in-law, mishaps were an every day occurrence so it might as well be for the sake of science since nobody else is paying any attention.

There followed other experiments where cats served as the most direct and most cost effective medium. As mere farmkids we understood better how the Presidency and the Joint Chiefs understood their position in any national emergency. We too gave Congressional Medals of Honor to posthumous cats. When a cat died, we held parades for these heroic cats and their name was written on the cement staves of the silo which, even if the guaranteed immortality failed, they still had their name written in orange crayon on the silo wall. Should there be a snag in than guaranteed hereafter, their name in orange crayon was still better off than what happened to most cats.

Some survived despite our technique, and with practice plus the addition of strategic padding the reentry vehicle was improved and these cats became famous in their own time. They were allowed the hallowed position on the warm spot of the vacuum pump and got the milk strainer pad which they ate whole. Often as not this killed them outright but fame is like that.

That there were kids who became farmers instead of astronauts and politicians and generals and even a few who might have become saints, is all because the preliminary experiments were conducted on cats. If the sudden stop didn't hurt the cat it was probably worth a try yourself. If the fame of a cat spoiled it so that it became fat and lazy and mean at the milk dish, then maybe that wasn't worth a farmkid to try either.

Wood Fire

Some there are, made of wood. People and kinds, tribes and colonies... made of wood; all of them Pinocchios, more of wood than flesh and blood.

I was raised and tutored in the sacred circle of wood, its commandment was simple, to do wood well and abundantly, or die. By this lesson did we know all the wonderful and violent instruments... axes — single, double and kindling. Too there was the pole axe used to kill cattle without wasting powder or making noise as to scare away lactation at the other end of the barn. Various other hatchets: the claw hatchet for turning over logs, the shingle hatchet with a hammer on the back, and our Boy Scout tomahawk. Where Jim Bowie and Texas presumed their ironing-board size knife was central to survival, we the wild childs of Wisconsin knew a Bowie knife wasn't but an oversized chrome bumper meant to frighten tourists. It was overdone. What the right farm bairn carried was a "stick edge," a hatchet with a slim face and a square back end. Carry this tomahawk in the woods and you never get lost, never freeze to death, never fail to set fire, never feel alone or unarmed. As a Boy Scout in the care of the Rattlesnake Patrol, each member carried as our sign a limbing hatchet, made up from the loose head bin at the Army surplus store for 58 cents each. To this vagabond edge we attached a blue beech handle of our own making, but only after it had dried awhile behind the furnace. The handle once fit and socketed to the blade was soaked in a bucket of water overnight. The head never ever come off. On the handle we inscribed our secret Boy Scout names and the legend, "member of the Rattlesnake Patrol."

If the Arthur's child was stood up and made brave by Excaliber, if Wallace was given spine by the claymore, if Lee and Grant had their cavalry swords, if Armstrong Custer's was in sterling silver, our emblem of utmost was the Rattlesnake Patrol tomahawk, of blue beech cured a month behind the stove. In the woods our task was to gain a sufficient mountain of firewood to defend the farmhouse through the winter, as piles go it was not an inconsiderate heap. Our chore became a casual routine duty to which the farm employed three woodsteads. The highland woods was oak mostly, another had the character of red maple, birch and ash with some elms sufficiently lofty to serve as God's easy chair. The swamp was balsam, basswood and cedar and only sorta firewood.

Ours was the classic method of working the woods, logging trails ventured throughout the lot, an intricate maze of trails, on whose narrow, contorted paths we toured our skidding tractor. A narrow-front Allis Chalmers, hand cranked with a bedpan driver's seat. The engine block was cracked and leaked coolant so we dosed it with cornmeal every now and again to plug the leak. Tractor didn't seem to mind and didn't leak for quite some while in between and when it did, was redosed with corn meal. In the toolbox was a tobacco can of yellow cornmeal, only a tobacco can sealed tight against mice who'd have a nest in that toolbox in the space of a day using newsprint and seat cushions from god-knows-where and there dwell like fine and feudal lords. In the Allis Chalmers toolbox. It may have been the smell of cornmeal that attracted them in the first place. Even when we finally brazed the hole in the engine block, the mice continued to make their nests in the toolbox. Perhaps the scent of the cornmeal lingers. Maybe it was just a nice place. The factory did provide the access hole, the intent of the engineers was an allowance for the grease gun, so its extended pipette could protrude out that hole. They hadn't figured into the design the amperage of the deer mouse on the standard farm. Whose will is to find every good and comfortable vestibule available on the farmstead and fill it with nest. Initially, the toolbox nests were rudely dislocated and thrown out until one particular cold day we had forgotten to bring a bundle of newspapers to start the swamp fire, around whose single cheer was our willing service convened. A mouse nest we discovered has even better flammable properties than newsprint alone. Due probably to the mix of paper, chewed seat cushion and semi-oily mouse hair. We never again threw mouse nests away.

The exacting element of the Allis Chalmers WC was the narrow front wheels. A tractor that could for all intents be steered at a right angle, equal in agility to any bulldozer and ten times as fast. This tractor was our woods snake, the Allis Chalmers WC narrow front, if not quite as nimble as a horse it was faster and entirely indefatigable, so long as we remembered the cornmeal.

The woodlots of the farm were honeycombed and labyrinthed. Infested with contorted, double-jointed trails, miles of lanes that soon disappeared from view, dodging trees, cradle knolls, spring holes. To this roundup of firewood was our early winter devoted, like cowboys we were, instead of roping spring heifers or mustangs we gathered up windfalls, lightning-struck, the over-crowded, each sawn into lengths of a size the WC could tow, the snow of the trail became packed and solidified into a glide path of frictionless zeal. The logs and limbs were trailed to the wood yard at some central spot where a fire was burning, there the logs and boughs were delimbed and cut into short bolts, which is to say liftable lengths, the branches thrown to the fire.

Always we kept a watch for handle-wood, there was then it seemed a shortage of handles; a shovel, pitchfork, pickaxe always in need of a new one. Hop hornbeam, muscle wood we called it, these were set aside to take home separate from the firewood. For more tomahawks of the kind issued to the members of the Rattlesnake Patrol. We went armed in those days. It was only right as we were sworn keepers of the woodlot. A little less than a knight was a woodskeeper, a soothsayer of trees a tenderness to the beasts, a savior of the shades. Not Matt Dillon, but something close by. Armed were we with the cutty axe, this tomahawk ever at our side. Was with this we blazed the tree about to die. Blazed the trail for the snake-agile tractor, limbed the log and fueled the warming fire. We lost them often and made another. My uncle from Des Plaines who admired tools paid three dollars for one. Later he returned it saying he wanted the official seal burned in the handle, saying, "member of the Rattlesnake." Accomplished with a flat nail heated at the kitchen stove. We were then more of wood made than flesh and blood. It was warm-blood.

No Merit Badge
Was Offered

The Rattlesnake Patrol was a mutant form of the Boy Scouts. At least that is where it all started, at regulation Boy Scouts — khaki uniform, merit badge, and the official neckerchief slide from the official catalog. The Rattlesnake Patrol was an offshoot, how far off is hard to say. It was composed entirely of farmkids except for Bernie, whose dad owned the wrecking yard. On Saturday afternoons in winter we'd help him burn out cars to be recycled, in sooty, sometimes unquenchable fire, for this the Boy Scouts of America did offer no merit badge. Was Bernie who taught us a skill that later proved provident, the acetylene torch method of spare parts. For this neither was there a merit badge.

The Scouts did offer a merit badge for canoeing, swimming, archery, fire starting, stamp collecting, lawn care; it did not offer a merit badge for haying, silo filling, bagging potatoes, barn cleaning, firewood, milking cows or burning the marsh, as explains why the Rattlesnake Patrol was different, because our lives were different.

Every spring the Samoset Council sponsored a collective camp-out beside a glacial pothole in the northwest corner of Portage County. Rarely did the Rattlesnake

Patrol participate because the outing routinely coincided with spring field work and the chief objective of
that moment was the installation of the potato crop,
whose planting required a kind of devotion consistent
with the Lenten season. It was a shared ritual followed
by every member of the family during a period of forty
days. Sometimes it was fifty, sixty; potatoes are like that.
Every spare hour was spent attending to this ancestral
cloistered worship.

Lengthwise and across. That is what we called it,
lengthwise and across. The Latin is *longitudinem et transgredi,* and just so coincidentally the very same motion
favored over the foretrunk of Catholics, this what we
practiced secretly. Methodists in the dim light of the cellar, cloistered, length and across, Catholics. Every spring,
Catholics. Lengthwise and across. Holy Roman Potato
Catholics. Thus were we anointed by the holy 40 days
and 40 nights, keeping to the ever steady motion known
to our fathers and their fathers before and those on and
on unto unspeakable and distant time all the way back to
Saint Francis, who it was gave us the sacred order. Saint
and Sir Francis Drake to be exact, good rogue and servant
to the frecked queen. Was he, Saint and sinner Francis,
who stole the potato, not an auspicious beginning, this
from the Spaniards, who in turn stole it from the Incas, to
whose glory we ever-after celebrated during the Lenten
season, and to it and him our lives were devoted.

Lengthwise and across, this the cutting action to render to seed otherwise regular potatoes. Lengthwise and
across an ash board in the middle of where protruded a
fine honed butcher knife. Honed was this knife to paper
thin as cut molecules in half as happen to lean against
it. Lengthwise and across, an hour before school, before
barn chores, after chores, before supper, after supper.
Took an hour for us in our tight chill knot to cut what

a modern mechanical cutter does in 60 seconds, maybe 30. Lengthwise and across. Beautiful Catholics we were. Trained to a regular beat and rigor of devotion rare seen outside the laboratory. All to prosper the potato, lengthwise and across, lengthwise and across. *Longitudinem et transgredi.*

A variable thing is spring in the northern tier. March often proves snowy and cold, as it sometimes proves other. Potato planting follows these variable tides of spring, pulled two weeks early one year, two weeks late another. On this one particular year the season ran late, so our fathers said we, the Rattlesnake Patrol, could attend the Grand Assembly and Potlatch of the Samoset Council held every spring at a genuine, regulation, authorized and official Boy Scout campsite. It was an almost delirious sense of normalcy, one we rarely experienced.

Our anticipation of attending this Rendezvous was quite unbounded and enthusiastic. For this we prepared ourselves and engineered from a former silage wagon canvas a teepee standing a full 18-foot to the smoke hole and nine foot across. The canvas had seen better days as explains how we came by it in the first place, the trimmed pieces were used to patch the holes that rendered it unserviceable even to cover hay, but good enough for Boy Scouts. At least the Rattlesnake Patrol. It weighed 80 pounds dry, the poles, all 14, were peeled ash, themselves none too light. Our solution when presented with this problem of overburden was to fashion from a former milk can carrier a tent cart to whit we socketed one pole for a tongue and piled on the remaining poles and thereafter the teepee. It looked novel and not entirely authentic of the prairie culture, which is why I suppose no merit badge was offered.

The weekend of the Grand Encampment coincided with one of those March blizzards that some otherwise

calm persons describe as heinous, and some small if not
infinitesimal minority think of as heroic. We as farmkids were used to being part of the infinitesimal in most
considerations, as explains also the Rattlesnake Patrol.
The evening before the wind had turned the roads too
hazardous to travel. Except the pothole was on the way
to Amherst Junction feed mill and with 18 hundred-
weight of ground feed on its hind end, the farm pickup
was equal to just about anything March cared to try. We,
the Rattlesnake Patrol, arrived at the official camp-out
site to find the place deserted except for a handwritten
sign posted at the front gate. Due to weather, the notice
declared, the scheduled event was canceled. Our father
at this very juncture disappearing into the distance with
the pickup well loaded with new ground feed. Happy
to be rid of us and our contraption teepee.

Perhaps it was knowing we might not soon get another
opportunity to attend an official Boy Scout Camp including of merit badge qualification, that we decided not to
attempt a phone call from a neighboring farm. Perhaps
it was knowing that a blizzard as could shut down the
camp-out would not similarly shut down farm chores.
We erected our teepee in the lee of some concealing hem-
locks, gathered firewood and put by our food box filled
with two whole chickens, a slab of bacon, flour, baking
powder, potatoes (of course), butter, three loaves of Ma's
bread, about four dozen eggs and one jar of jam, it was
strawberry.

The wind rose and the snow continued. Snowed like
it does in March, mostly sideways snow. The curious
thing is how come any of it ever does land on the ground
with all that energy spent on sideways. By Saturday
morning there was a foot of newly threshed snow over
the sand counties. The town roads were impassable,
county roads similarly and US 51 was empty and still

in both directions as is a pleasant and remarkable sight. As is with sideways snow, the measurement of the 12 inches is disproportionately distributed, some places quite bare while others are artistically inundated. An example of this phenomenon we had on the farm was a hollow cove between the milkhouse and the barn which the wind when from a particular westerly direction filled with snow, despite the rest of the farmyard remained empty. A three-inch snowfall might in its entirety end up in that hollow juncture between the milkhouse and the double thick barn door. My grandfather thought it because he had omitted to bury the severed head of a rooster under the concrete slab between the barn door and the milkhouse. My father admonished the idea, saying that it was instead aerodynamics as did it. To which my grandfather replied, that is precisely what he said. Rooster aerodynamics.

It was a luxuriant two days and nights at the official Boy Scout Campout. We ate well, tended the fire and read the books we brought: *Last of the Mohicans*, the journal of Frances Parkman and *Peyton Place*. A good thing is life when snowbound, the simple chore of tending the fire nourished us as surely as did the potatoes baked in the coals. We hiked over the drifts to the New Hope cemetery and listened in the lee of those stones to the howl of Norwegian ghosts. It was no easy matter to tell whether those were Norwegian ghosts who howled and not just your average Pollock or Welsh ghosts, but we supposed ghosts were homeward elements and didn't go traipsing about howling at foreign folk cemeteries. Then we hiked back to our teepee and made tea of pine needles and read some more. We were inspired to make a lamp of bacon grease and a sock, it burned well and provided a nice aroma. A passage from Parkman encouraged us to fashion a peace pipe of sumac whose pith we burned out with a length of barbwire heated in the fire. Took three hours to gain a reasonable facsimile, arguing the while over whether right Indian tobacco is more redbark and willow or more redbark and sweet fern. We tried both blends, the sweet fern seemed too chewy for true ceremonial smoke. Again I believe there is no merit badge offered for this.

My father found us late on Sunday afternoon, the tee-pee was down in a minute and dragged back to the pickup truck. Twice he observed we might have camped closer to the road. We were home in time for evening chores, need I mention no merit badge is offered.

O'ercrow

On the farm a variety of terms were available to describe the ability to see from some increased elevation. A neighbor could be said to have the sight of tractor seat high. From it the sense of his character, his philosophy being some better than a person whose world view, whose sense of insight and prophecy was only kitchen chair high. So there were variations of this; silo high was some better than roof-up, ridge row up was some better perspective than hop pole high. Mow-up refers to that look of the farmstead from the height of the mow door. This was an appropriate perch if one's duty is as the sniper deployed to frustrate cats. Weaponry can vary; slingshot, B-B gun, a bushel of B size potatoes. Success was the benefit of this perch. Cats ordinarily do not look up so it is a fine thing to bother them from a place they don't suspect. The sensation is what it must be like to torment the victim of a psychosis, neither the cat nor the psychotic can see where all their trouble is coming from.

Tree-up is higher than mow-up. Mow-up meant no more than climbing the oak rungs into the mow and looking out the hay door, as a corpse can do. Tree-up takes a little more adventure and maybe better muscle tone, depending on the tree. A boxelder is an easier tree to climb than an oak, maple generally were that companionable, but the best kind were pines — white, red and balsam fir. It seemed to us they were less trees than living ladders, so easy, so available were the rungs of them to climb. The essential effort here is to get a firm grip, hug up your entrails, and claw your way up that tree. Tree-up is good vantage for looking over sheds, ice houses, fences. Hunters use tree-up to kill deer 'cause deer, like cats, ain't commonly inclined to look up. Neither is anything else, except religion, which accounts for its own kind of troubles. So much looking up that the most common thing becomes a dangerous obstacle.

Barn-up is the view from the ridge row of the barn. Before all those blue enamel silos, this was as high as the ordinary country stick could get. Hunting from barn-up proved useless to most farmers. Maybe you can see well enough but the size of the target wasn't improved by being situated on the barn roof. Never mind gun shots didn't do Holstein lactation any good. Barn-up is a good place for eyeing the wet spot in the field and checking on the young stock back by the creek. At barn-up, the view is over 95 percent of the things that fly, like pigeons, swallows, sparrows and starlings. This alone makes barn-up the special place it is, as good a sight as any bird; well, mostly any bird. Doesn't get any better than barn-up, least not without raising the ante of personal risk.

After barn-up there was only one place more, unless you were riding a rocket or climbing Mt. Everest, and that is o'ercrow. Before the arrival of the blue Harvestors, the chance to o'ercrow was limited to climbing white pine trees and-or scaling the sandstone ledge below Bancroft. The ledge is fine place to o'ercrow but not what is termed handy when a person wants a dose of overview. Strange need it was, o'ercrow. Sometimes it felt like an addiction so powerful was the need. It hit on a yearning so hard I wanted to climb before supper. Before wanting to sleep and drink Kool-Aid or read my copy of *Peyton Place* I wanted to o'ercrow. No reason other than just wanting it, which I guess qualifies as an addiction. Nothing else would do. It seemed as if I had to get off the ground, get up among the ethers to be and feel free, get up so high I wasn't tempted to blast cats with a B-B gun, ain't a more sincere moment in a kid's life. Get up in a tree so high all there was left to do was hold on and think. The tree has gotta be white pine, else it ain't o'ercrow. At a time like this you don't want anything in the way of a deliberate climb, tight sneakers and clean underwear are necessities. Loose Keds don't hold and underwear going crosswise half way up a tree is downright dangerous. You ain't at o'ercrow till you arrived at the last stick of wood on the tree capable of supporting your weight if you don't wiggle. O'ercrow is just one branch lower than the one that would break if you sat on it. A climb like this is a sterling moment in any kid's life. About as close to hallucinating as you can get without smoking Cuban cigars. A person's intestine turns into a garden hose just thinking about o'ercrow and some can't get beyond thinking how big a dent you'd make if you fall. They forget from this height you will burn up in the atmosphere before even hitting the ground. As a kid I studied trees for a long time, not knowing whether I ought to try at them. And if I did, whether I ought wear new Keds or old Keds. New Keds had a better grip, but if your ma buys them like mine does, the new pair has a hole you are expected to fill in with your foot sometime in the next six weeks but don't yet fit. So the shoe is looser than it should be for a kid about to climb halfway to the moon. As ain't the climbing apparatus necessary for o'ercrow. Sometimes I had everything ready and I walked away from the tree 'cause the fear of climbing all the way to o'ercrow melted my fingers to where they were blunt and rounded off and not the talons required. The wind is another thing. You don't want to go o'ercrow when the tree is sweeping the sky like a Sunday morning broom and the sky ain't the least bit dirty and the tree sweeping all the same like a crazy old woman. O'ercrow on a day like this on a tree like that, is plain suicide. Well, maybe not actual intentional done-up suicide but close enough as to be only arguing over the caliber.

O'ercrow like I said is the last sure limb on the tree. Ain't ever been a kid who reached o'ercrow didn't know for himself the vision of angels, what angels have all the time. I lived the whole length of my child time in the sand flats west of the moraine and o'ercrow on that sort of flat real estate is exactly heaven, and nothing is fairer than the sight of the fields spreading out beneath my Keds. Field connected to field, field to woods, farms dotting the land as far as the eye can see. At this height you can't smell chores, the headlines on the newspaper don't matter, what year it is doesn't matter. What matters is that peaceful land, the green of the pastures, the contentment of cows. Seeing this I was no longer a kid, if not quite god I was something with wings and that sense felt as good as I suspect there was good to be had.

As a kid in the tree I doubted the Bible, where it said Man were the image and spittin' image of the Big Guy when it looked for all intents and purposes the crow had the best option. To my mind, dress-up funerals, college diplomas and flannel pajamas don't make up for that a crow can look down on more earth than any saint or preacher in world history, and without the encumbrance of stairs. At that moment in that tree I was sorely tempted to trade off the whole painted-up noisy gosh darn of humanity for being a crow. O'ercrow in the pine tree caused me to understand that humanity was at best second place;

nice though it was, still second place.

I ain't been o'ercrow so often as to spoil it. Most of the time being human ain't so bad as long as when the mood strikes me there's a white pine tree nearby and I can climb right out of my human skin and take on wings for a while, at the place we once called o'ercrow.

Mandan Nights

My grandfather had a leather bound copy of the *Journal of Merriwether Lewis,* the book sequestered in the oak secretary stained to such a dark hue it resembled obsidian more than wood. Two low shelves contained his library, six linear feet of books. Cozily assembled here was the King James, *Little Women, The Lincoln Dictionary, Tarzan,* a first edition, *History of China,* Marco Polo's biography, same for T. Roosevelt, a volume of Shakespeare's plays, Burns' poems, an edition of collected sermons, the *Handbook for Midwestern Agriculture, Ten Notable Women, Home & Farm Surgery,* General Grant's memoirs, *The Horsemanship and Blacksmith Journal,* and the *Journal of Meriwether Lewis.*

My grandfather did brag sometimes that we were kinsmen to McKay who was with MacKensie to the Columbia in service of the Northwest Company, the very same mentioned in the journal of Meriwether. I began reading the journals not because Meriwether was the first to see the badger or the Nez Perce Indians, but to find the cousin by name of McKay who emigrated eventually to Wisconsin where he dropped the prefix and became plain Kays. I was 12. And being what 12 meant on the farm. I milked cows every night after school, belonged to Boy Scouts, 4-H, MYF. Peddled potatoes door to door in Neenah, Menasha, Appleton. Potatoes we raised and picked by hand and in a good day could and did make more money, peddling potatoes door to door, than did the dairy of 45 Holsteins. I drove the farm truck on the back roads, spent my summers aboard a tractor. Swam at the pit, read science fiction, anything to do with rockets, tented Saturday nights in the back woods. I believed girls were superior sorts of animals same as crows, I swam naked at the irrigation pit in the summer twilight, came home smelling of algae and frogs. I read later into the night than was wise on a bed with a cottonseed mattress, and gazed longingly at the lingerie ads in the Monkey Ward catalogue, and here began reading Meriwether, this as I came to call him. Reading Meriwether was my reply when asked what I was up to when my room light ought be turned off. It felt good to be on a first name basis with a major contributor to American history, never mind MacKensie had beat Meriwether to the Columbia by four years.

I was 13 when I hit the upper Missouri with Meriwether in the winter of 1804-05, and I too spent the winter with the Mandan between going to school for Mrs. Ross and being a Boy Scout and doing barn chores and chicken coop chores and woodshed chores and haying and skatin' on the irrigation pit and building rockets out of salt peter and ether cans. The rest of the time I was wrapped in my grandma's quilt, in an over-stuffed chair in the corner of her parlor, somewhere up the Missouri with Meriwether.

I loved the Mandan better than the Methodists and would have traded in a second my kirk baptism for whatever was their formula. I woulda traded in my white chance of living 85 years for a chance at being Mandan and dying of smallpox at 16. Was an obvious trade, like marbles for a jackknife, chewing gum for fircrackers; least it seemed obvious to me.

For a kid, I was smarter than I looked. I doubted God. I wondered how God coulda let the dinosaurs die when they were so beautiful and interesting, and how come God didn't preserve the Mandan when he coulda saved them the same as Israel, didn't strike me as the least bit fair. When I was 13 I talked with God about his screw-ups and playing favorites and playing dirty tricks on innocent people and animals and even trees. I suspected God was a coward; later as a seminarian I learned this wasn't quite the right language to couch the sentiment.

As a kid I knew the Mandan village in the country of the upper Missouri was the finest human habitation ever conceived by mortal man; simple, cheap, durable, warm. They were without question the best-off people on the planet, save maybe Tahiti, and Frank Lloyd Wright, whose book I read. Wright I thought was a stuffed shirt who knew nothing whatsoever about how to make a house; a building maybe, but not a house. A house that could watch and tend the landscape and arise from the materials as the land provided. The Mandan lived in packed earth lodges that held a family and several layers of cousins. Less than a barn, more like a chicken coop, they were oval-shaped blisters, weatherproof, snug, with a central smoke hole, a common area for eating, cooking and entertainment, and private family sections to the side where people slept. The Mandan lodge was no drafty wigwam but futuristic like Buckminster Fuller, and nicely warm despite being in North Dakota. Neat as the castles of England and Scotland, except the Mandan were warm.

With adolescence I found the Mandan even more interesting; I reread numerous entries in Meriwether's journal. January ... "Four days now we have celebrated the new year, one night at Living Dog's, another at Black

Cat's, another at Steaming Water. Some of the men are quite depleted from the many wives of the warriors offered to them on seccessive nights." Meriwether meant sex. If my mama knew where Meriwether was going, and it wasn't just to find the Northwest Passage, she'da burned that book. Meriwether went on, " ... the Mandan believe the prowess and greatness of one man is transferrable to another by using the wife as an intermediary to convey the subject essence."

Meriwether did not mention whether the Mandan squaws were pretty or not, apparently it didn't matter; I was 13 and understood. What impressed me was Meriwether wrote of it honest, the same as every other observation he made. I learned this is a rare thing for literature. No Romeo and Juliet, no sappy letters, no deceptions; just honest animal adoration in the warm winter lodge of the Mandan.

I wondered if my grandfather ever read the journal of Meriwether Lewis or if it was just another fat book on the shelf. I wondered if he too wished the smallpox hadn't wiped them out and there was somewhere west of the St. Croix, west of Minneapolis, west of St. Cloud was a prairie kind whose habitations were warm, simple and cheap. Who could have taught Frank Lloyd Wright a thing or two.

The Version
According to James

*And the Lord God planted a garden eastward unto Eden;
and there he put the man whom he had formed.*

*And out of the ground made the Lord God to grow every
tree that is pleasant to sight and good for food; the tree of life
also in the midst of the garden, and the tree of knowledge of
good and evil.*

— Genesis 28:8-9, according to the version
of James of Scotland, England and Virginia

Shortly before my grandfather's death, when he
was still lucid and alive, a visitor presented to him
a version of the Bible in the New English. He read
several chapters from it and then said to my grandmother
to put the book away, for it was in a wrongful tongue. Its
language, he said did not rise with a mighty spine and
make you marvel. Put it away, he said. Put it away.

Some years later I asked my grandmother why there
was under the leg of her kitchen table a book. She replied
the book was there to level out the table being the foot
had broken off. The book was there to level it out.

I observed to my grandmother that a block of wood

might serve the purpose. She replying that the book was
serving penitence.
The book with the red covers? I asked.
The very one.
But it is a new book.
It is, came her reply.
But grandmother, I exclaimed, the book has not only
nice red covers and not only is it new and the pages crisp
but, Grandmother, the book is the Bible.
Is it now? she responded.
Yes I can see under the stump of the table leg, it says
The Holy Bible, in gold letters.
Does it say King James somewhere there also?
Not that I can see.
Then it is not the Bible.
But grandmother, on the cover it says the Ho...
Child, it is mistaken.

.   .   .

My lessons in language and what is language's power
to invoke began when I was a child in the tend of the
Methodist kirk. For there every Sunday did the god-
speak utter words according to James of Scotland, Ireland,
England and Wales, also the Champagne region of France.
This the same language that Shakespeare wrote, the same
of Elizabeth the Queen and Defender, love object of Sir
Walter Raleigh, befriender of Drake, captain of the Golden
Hind, she red haired and freckled, she who put Mary
Queen of Scots to the block who was Rome and besides
a trouble-maker as were the Scots generally, whose reign
when ended was supplanted by James I of Scotland, the
very offspring of Mary the beheaded, who came to the
throne as James VI a Protestant, a follower of witches and
necromancer, this the like tendency of Scots, and under
whose authority, coin and promise came the canticle according to the realm of words as was upon this fair and

English time. Spain was in decline, the first Holocaust of the Inquisition nearing an end, Galileo's glass had re-made the universe, this when James decreed the Empire should now have the Book according to its own mouth. Not text of Latin or Greek but of good English yew and Saxon soil shall this gospel belie.

I do not know what book and chapter it is surmised that William Shakespeare wrote, nor those verses as are rumored by the hand of James himself. I am inclined to listen to this book because the English, beyond taking up the flame of Luther against a church too proud, did dare a worse deed. Did commit the earnest sin and to make Book of the vulgar tongue. Rare in the millennium and two hundred since the Council at Nicaea had the collected essays been offered in a tribal format.

In the township of Buena Vista when the wizened Reverend Feldt rose in the north pulpit of the Liberty Corners for a scripture lesson to farmers under whose arms and elbows I did dwell, and lifted up in his melancholy pallor the verbs of Moses and David, Solomon and Tobit, I did hear it my own born tongue. In rumbling, roaring, Shakepole English, London-town and Francis Drake, the pirateer, the Great Armada and blood-stained Tower. Read from the book of James who very feared witches and wrote scripture with quill pen, mistranslating the whole while.

As a farmers' bairn did I believe. If not so much in Jesus the carpenter's boy resurrected from the dead, if not so much in the Passover of the Angel of Death, not of heaven and hell awaiting, but did I believe for the last best reason. A belief in words. The power of words said and written to raise hope, find faith, hold a family, tend both the farmer and those in peril. Despite their extinction is certain, and their death to go un-noted, they by the spine of these words are lifted above mere life, even to everlasting, raised up by words familiar and fair, words experienced and words knowing. Though doom be inevitable, the lesson of language is greater than the end. By the story told in the guise of its own place is the home of the gods revealed, the spark always to wake again. The ash to stir, the dust will murmur, the mud boil and then where light is provoked and we shall again be, and the darkness smile.

The good reverend then bowed his bald pate, closed the version of James and said amen to the words according to my tribe.

Dirtball Shoes

When I was in high school the lowest form of life was the dirtball. Kids of the present age call each other names — jerk, pencil neck, dweb and nerd — as once it was dirtball, hayseed, hick and most loathsome of all... farmer.

Occasionally I still hear these honored epithets. Not long ago a neighbor related how she was worried her son was becoming a dirtball. I asked her what exactly is a dirtball. It's hard to say, she said. Peculiar behavior mostly, like wearing those gopher-stomping boots. How he wants a pickup truck when he is old enough to drive. Listens endlessly to country music, owns three cowboy hats, has a pair of boots with silver toes and thinks none too well of college prep. I had to agree... sure signs of a dirtball.

I suspect the current definition comes close to what was a dirtball 40 years ago when I was a plebe to that fraternity of esquires. Then it was eight-inch high tops in ox-blood worn to school where a decent college preppie wore penny loafers or black caddies with the spring closure. Eventually when I went to college I did own a pair of penny loafers in order to blend in with the natives, despite my personal preference was still for eight-inch ox-blood farm shoes, for reason of pure comfort. However, I knew I would never get laid wearing farmer shoes except by some female gorilla from the College of Natural Resources, when I had my sights set on something more definitively female. Maybe even someone who shaved her legs.

Had I been born to the current generation, I might have worn hightops to class and demonstrated my political outlook. Country shoes are now altogether correct being they are ecologically minded. My daughter wore hiking boots her entire college career and nobody associated her with genuine dirt.

Shoes, it seems to me, are the dead giveaway to a person's identity, declaring with precision their values in life, how far off the pavement they are willing to venture, their politics, like as not their household budget, and whether or not they possess any inherent dirtball potential. I have worn all manner of shoes during my various sojourns and none of them has the sense of secure attachment to earth as a pair of eight-inch high tops.

Most Americans believe the cowboy boot is the true epicenter of the dirtball cosmos; they are mistaken. Cowboy boots are to farmer shoes what insulated Sorrel boots are to Nike basketball shoes... about the same volume and size but you can't slam dunk wearing snowmobile boots. Don't get me wrong, I like cowboy boots. They are attractive, come handsomely tooled and when wearing a pair of these I am significantly taller for one who can otherwise pass for one of Santa's elves.

These benefits aside, it is not possible to do real work wearing cowboy boots. About the only concession I'll grant cowboy boots is they are faster on the draw by several minutes when it comes to skinnying at the creek or where else skinnying makes sense. Meaning cowboy boots occupy the same moral dimension in the shoe business as sandals. 'Cause if you're in that much of a hurry, like as not you're swimming in somebody else's pond. Also, it is darn obvious guys who wear cowboy boots are lousy lovers 'cause anybody in such an all-fired hurry isn't like to get the pilot light lit first. A farmer who has learned to unlace high tops a hole at a time is far more capable of bringing a female to working pressure before letting out the clutch. High tops are as a consequence a good matrimonial instinct, though I am tempted to say... aid.

Then there's plowed ground. New plowing is the only earth form and/or condition known to have a true negative pressure. They will suck cowboy boots right off the bottom of a foot at any velocity over one mile per hour, which ain't velocity enough to head off the heifers. Some folks think sneaker types are the implement for such a situation but are only theorizing 'cause if they ever tried sneaky shoes they'd realize they get shucked off by new plowing almost as quick as cowboy boots.

I have absolutely no faith in Jesus shoes. When I see a person wearing sandals I know this person is either (A) useless to mankind because you can't do a lick of work in sandals or (B) they are filthy rich. Myself, I would have more respect for the New Testament if it weren't postulated by so many folks wearing sandals.

I have worn high tops since birth. Farmer shoes my darling wife calls them. Eight inches high with speed hooks at the last four stations. If I am in a hurry I simply tie them off at the last hole level and get going, though the laces drag some. A pair of Red Wings lasts me two years if I don't happen to catch them in an auger or something in an equally bad mood. Ordinarily this is dangerous; not however when I am wearing dirtball boots. I have stopped stampedes with those shoes, quit prairie fires, torn down buildings, eradicated cubic miles of taters and kick-started diesel engines. A while back a carpenter friend told me about a tool for taking boards off an old barn. I told him I already had such, raising my dread tread up about eye level for him to see. Just scrunch yourself in the bucket of a front end loader and mule those boards off. Sometimes using the right tool in the right place is about as satisfying as a thing gets.

Every once in awhile on a Sunday afternoon I sin, I wear tennis shoes to the shop to catch up on some welding. Splatter I don't ordinarily notice lands on my shoes, melts through and again I learn why tennis shoes are a sin.

Saturday morning the first thing I do at the farm shop is fetch the can of dab, and before doing a lick of work, smear my shoes with a new coat of ox blood. Every Saturday morning the same. Same as my father did, same as his dad before. The chore done, the shoes look most new 'cept where something or other took a bite. Polishing shoes is the same as bathing and sex: once a week whether you need it or not.

I have mentioned at other times how I'd like to set up a farmer's Hall of Fame. In it I'd have cast iron statues of famous farm junk, stuff that has combined to make farming more entertaining, if not easier, than it has a right to be. Stuff like a front porch complete with farm dog, bib overalls, jackknife, toothpick, center pivot, hydraulic ram, and them … them farmer shoes… with the last four places being speed lacers… them eight-inch, ox-blood, high tops.

E ... lect ... Trick Fence

Science to a farmkid is a different thing than what is science class at school. Chicken killing and hog time were either gross hideous farm chores, or else they were large scale science projects that were a lot more interesting than the prostrate frog in Mr. Hager's biology class. As a kid I learned what makes science possible is attitude, where every disgusting and deplorable thing has scientific value if a person's attitude is upbeat or at least investigative.

I learned a lot of science from my dad's electric fence. I learned there are things even a nervous system in complete disarray can not by brute force adjourn, such as the cow's instinct for green corn. Especially warm August night milk-stage corn that says beautiful, non-verbal things somewhere in the central cortex of the cow's brain.

How it happened that my dad invested in the electric fence is because the five-strand barb wire drawn up to a tensile pitch didn't sufficiently interfere with green-corn neurons in the cow brain. The salesman said the alternating pulse electric fence will stop 'em dead in their tracks,

Won't quite kill 'em. Won't turn their milk to curd or cut up udders as will a tight-done five strand. Won't cost hardly nothing, save for insulators and a coil of aluminum wire. The salesman went on to say how a kid dumber than dirt can fence up 40 acres in less time than it takes to dig out the outhouse pit. For some reason this attribute appealed to my dad. All you do then is plug the main unit of the fencer into the wall socket, after which, he restated, it couldn't possibly kill the cow. Won't upset her digestion and it won't turn her into a kicker.

As all theologians know, there was only one way to prove any of this. The man told my dad to touch the demonstrator so he'd understand this device wasn't lethal to a milk cow. I remember my dad and the salesman sorta looked at each other the way grown-up people do who are considering doing something with six-guns in a public street. The sales guy wearing a suit coat and tie and my dad in his standard greasy overalls. The salesman, seeing something low down and pitiful in my dad, grabbed hold of the electrode himself, blinked a few extra times then let go. Grinning like he just then shook hands with John the Baptist himself. He immediately held out the electrode to my dad, who rubbed his chin one lingering moment longer than he ought if he was to win that wager that passed between their eyes. When Dad grabbed it, his eyes got wide, kinda like Moses sitting on the burning bush. I am proud to say my dad held that electrode a couple eternal seconds longer than a person ought to on the first try. The salesman moved his eyes to his shoes and coughed.

So what you think?

Works, my dad said. Yup, it sure does work. From where I was standing I could see the fur on the back of Dad's neck was kinda rigid and porcupine-like.

Soon after we strung electric fence to the 10-acre

pasture behind the barn, where we intended the cows to stay put at green-corn time. Expecting cows to have a workable conscience is, as every farmer knows, an unreasonable moral constraint. The conscience is an organ hidden down behind the stomach, as is the case with most creatures including the human kind. The inference here being the conscience is always in the shadow of the stomach, which is why you can find a Weight Watchers Local in just about any village and hamlet on the face of the earth. The lucky thing for society is the conscience, though behind the stomach, is somewhat out in front of a couple other organs as can kick up dirt any time after dark.

Easiest fence making we ever did, the electric was, and a wonder of science besides. We studied the fence later that very evening. First we touched it with a blade of grass, known to be a high ohm resistor. What we felt was something but not what I'd call ticklish. Next we tried a greener length of grass, followed after by leaves, string, rhubarb, corn silk. The clearest indicator of the true manner of the electric fence was rhubarb. After which we touched it in the flesh. Hello, Mamma… so that's what electric means! 600 volts at .001 amps is a very interesting sensation, like being infested all of a sudden with termites, all of 'em set to gnawing and squiggling at once.

Between the arc welder and the electric fence we learned a general theory of electricity. Lots of amps at very little voltage melts steel. Lots of voltage at very little amps sends cows to catechism. Put the two together and get your ticket stamped to join the ancestors.

The fun of an electric fence was to get a pair of real dry sneakers… drier-than-dirt sneakers as have been sitting over the furnace vent for two days straight… then dare the city cousin to a contest of hang-time. First you hold the wire, then they try. You still holding on after they tried twice, both times knocked to the ground.

One night for reasons unknown we peed on the electric fence. I do not know why. It seemed at the time a valid scientific perspective. I think we peed on a lot of things back then. Like after climbing a tall tree we peed from it. It seemed for some reason a noteworthy spectacle. We also did this from bicycles, I no longer remember exactly how. It was an act symbolic of our special freedom as farmkids, marking our place on earth the same as the wolf. Perhaps this is why we peed on the electric fence.

My brother is the father of girl children, no boy bairns at all. I sired a girl also, flame red hair, in fact road-flare-red and freckles enough to pave a dirt road. The family had its share of red hair before but the hue has generally been more polite. I tend to credit my burning bush daughter to that episode with the electric fence. The neighbor boy who was also there turned out to be sterile as a mouse-nest acorn. We were all there, doing it, simultaneously, no trickles allowed.

Science does not believe a person can feel their genes being warped. Science is wrong.

The Games We Used to Play

My brother and I were often detailed to chores that were not only boring they were suffocating. Boredom, though modern science doesn't seem to be agree, can kill. Boredom is highly toxic. It is incredibly contagious and most surely stunts a kid's growth.

We knew at an early age that the boredom of standard farm chores was toxic, somehow kids know the truth of science before parents. Chores, like milking cows, grinding feed, cleaning pens, were chores that arrived not in puddles and splashes but oceanic expanses of chores, vast and un-navigable hinterlands of chores. Of all chores, potato picking was the most cruel, twenty acres of potatoes and every damn tuberosity of it picked by hand. Without this potato patch we might have starved to death, but at least that was a nicer way to die than by twenty acres on your hands and knees.

In 1957 my brother and I pooled our resources. This was no mean feat for our parents like all good farm stock did not pay an allowance. Instead we were provided with the sadistic alternative: pickles. As might be guessed, one more chore. For sources of revenue we had several choices: we could sell potatoes, raise a steer, my brother tried carrots... eventually we did peddle potatoes door to door in metropolitan Oshkosh, Appleton, Neenah, Menasha... but that was in the future. In 1957 I was 11, my brother Gary was 9; every chore, even those with rumored money at the end, was boring, which is why they call it a chore in the first place.

What we bought for 95 cents was an *Information Please Almanac,* 912 pages of extreme stuff. This was the book that went with us to every chore, even those where gloves and barn rubbers were necessary. We took it to the pickle patch, we had it close when cleaning the barn, mowing hay, fixing fence, and from this almanac evolved a strange game, at least strange for children. First Gary rumbled through the almanac to find a question while I tended the manure fork. Then I'd find a question while he steered the fork. The game was simple: questions, arcane and rare questions, questions to ponder and rummage through, to puzzle over and figure out... anything to occupy our minds. Despite the apparent squalor of the circumstance, the almanac game dispelled the boredom. In fact it slew boredom. Chopped it up in such little pieces that there wasn't hardly a chore before us we didn't suddenly relish. The more odious it was the better we liked it. The farther the field, the bigger the field, the better off we were. This game wasn't something adults could understand. Besides, they might take away the almanac.

It was I admit a weird game for kids, if not so weird for kids thinking they might otherwise die of boredom. It was Gary's turn to ask the question: How many Congresses have there been from 1789 to 1957? At this point we began a collective discussion, mind while we are doing this we are also cleaning the calf pens and hip deep in slime you don't want to imagine. Except we weren't there at all, instead we are somewhere else. Where I do not know but it surely wasn't in a spring barn doing what most people'd rather die than try.

How many Congresses since 1789? Let's see, two year terms, 1789 to 1889 is a hundred years, 1889 to 1957 is ... 68 years ... 168 years, divide by two; 84th Congress.

Correct.

Then it was my turn with the almanac and Gary's turn with the fork. What color was the White House originally? Now anybody can see this is a trick question, which was allowed as long as it is interesting.

So, he the brother who eventuated law school says, you wouldn't ask unless this is a trick question or else the White House really was a different color. Correct?

Correct. Clarification was permitted. So when was it repainted?

1815 or '16.

That would be after the War of 1812?

Yup.

After the British burned it?

Yup.

So it was a different color before?

A further clue could be offered... it was in its natural state.

So the question then is what is the White House made of?

Oops... too big a clue.

My brother pondered, knit his brows, all while digging away at the calf pen... being a government building, I'd guess it was made of stone, granite from Maine ... so the White House was originally grey.

Final answer? (By the way, we invented that phrase in 1957, not ABC in 1999.)

You wouldn't say that unless I was wrong... One more clue please?

The stuff is cheaper stone than granite from Maine.

What's cheap stone ... another clue ...

Roche Cri.

Sandstone ... the White House originally was brown.

Correct.

Then it was Gary's turn with the Almanac and mine with the manure fork.

I don't remember how long our childhood was, farm chores have a tendency to lengthen the process. By my own estimate we were kids in the whereabouts of 300 years; as said, chores tend to lengthen the term. There are times when I think I'm still that farmkid because the chores are the same abiding companions as always.

We used up several Almanacs in the course of our careers We survived those chores and never again were bored to the point of asphyxiation because there was that question to answer, to ponder.

Where was Samuel Goldwyn born?

OK, so that is too easy.

What does the 1st Amendment to the Constitution protect?

Clue: It wasn't farmkids.

Racer

Central Wisconsin, as everyone knows, is mountainous. We have here alpine meadows as lovely as Switzerland. Unfortunately for the sake of tourism the mountains are deflated at the moment, though they once were as lofty and awesome as Alps. The glaciers didn't help, bulldozing the rubble of what were once mountains into lumpy cottage-cheese kinds of formations. In my childhood the farm was on the peneplain, this Latin word meaning "most patient." That is what central Wisconsin looks like... something most patient.

It was that my married sister for my birthday gave me a pair of aviator goggles. I was eight. They were probably not precise aviator goggles as they had the kind of heavy duty frame and bulbous eyepieces more consistent with welder's goggles. But for me they were exact enough to be aviator goggles, or even better for my hope, racer's goggles.

I do not know why but I was at this early age a ready and prefabricated racer. My bicycle I had disassembled from its robust Schwinn countenance to become a flame-hued ezekiel shorn of fenders, horn-tank, book rack, basket, bell, light and handlebar pads. Even the rubber cleats on the pedals I had filed off with a rasp to lighten this bike. That it might, dear god almighty, pass the extreme barrier of 25 mph, and the known world record for a single speed Schwinn propelled by an eight year old across the vast inexhaustible peneplain. This the record for a distance of one mile, the exact same from the mailbox road to the first marsh bridge. It happened that the last quarter mile of the road was in native sand. The sand as made the record speed of 25 mph the more meaningful. Twenty-five mph is ever so easy on a concrete road, but the same velocity has world record implications on a sand road. Not gravel, not hard dirt, but sand… sandbox sand, barnyard sand, fat bike tire sand.

By eight years old I knew all about speed, the various classifications and the nuances. Chuck Yeager at the time was pursuing the speed barrier in the X-1 compliments of a rocket engine and a good head start, this from a B-29. I too might have attempted the sound barrier had the Air Force permitted me use of a B-29 and a few surplus rocket motors. Requiring nothing so fancy as an X-plane, instead a standard cow watering tank, attached in turn to a sheet of galvanized roofing, this altogether connected to the surplus rocket engine. Had I available to me then certain grant-writing credentials I think it entirely conceivable that I might have become the first eight year old to crack the sound barrier and accomplish the feat a lot cheaper than did Chuck Yeager. I do admit a galvanized stock tank hanging from the ceiling of the Smithsonian is not nearly so incredible or enthralling a display as Chuck Yeager's orange X-1. Still… by attaching a military grade nose cone and a bevy of instruments with official looking insignias, even a stock tank could quickly fit the documentable-look required of high velocity.

Which is why I painted my bike red. Red was well known to be a fast color, never mind it was barn paint. Red is inherently faster than the original purple in which my Schwinn arrived. Purple is a slow color. Ladies in purple move slower than ladies in yellow, I know this because I did the research. People in black move even slower than people in purple, again, the scientific reason why this should be is unknown, but it is observationally true. Which is why I painted my bike red, barn red. I would have preferred yellow but we didn't have yellow paint because nothing on the farm was yet yellow. John Deere tractors came later.

The useful thing about speed is it acts as a natural insult to mathematics. At eight years, I was in school just approaching two place addition, multiplication was yet a year away, algebra five years distant. At the art of math I was not particularly stellar or even necessarily buoyant except where that math involved itself with speed. I did not enjoy great success adding 39 to 43 but I was aware and animated by the 1,100 ft/sec as was the goal of Chuck Yeager. Though by adding the loss of air density at 23,000, the figure is closer to 1,430 ft/sec. I knew that 25 miles per hour over a one mile course was the elapsed time of 2 minutes, 24.26 seconds, the number gained from a quadratic equation comparing the known 60 mph to 88 ft/sec with the known 25 mile per hour to the unknown feet per second. Dividing 36.6 ft sec into 5280 = 144.262 seconds.

It took me and my bike most of the summer to finally accomplish the measure mile distance between the mail-box and the first creek in 2 minutes 24.262 seconds. The town road didn't then have a name other than it was out there somewhere on Route One. Never mind I had just entered the road into the record books the same as Chuck Yeager. His was the speed of sound; mine was 25 mph in sand. Was the sand end of the road that gave me all the trouble and I tried various tracks. The harder path was unfortunately the bumpiest and had more mud puddles.

Oddly I never told anybody how it was in the summer of '54 I achieved the hyperdyne velocity of 25 mph on a Schwinn over a one-mile length of town road, part paved, part not. The record I believe still stands in the eight year old Schwinn single speed class, this on a town road via their own quadratic equation. I remained somewhere between terrible and horrible at math in school, a solid citizen of B group for eight years straight. I now know why, because nobody attached math to a Schwinn, barn red paint and a pair of welder's goggles.

The Competition

A s a kid I knew every animal and bird had a different set of holes. Same as a saxophone has different holes than a flute, so a saxophone sounds different from a flute.

When we were butchering ducks, we cut out the voice box. Which probably wasn't a nice thing to do, never mind the duck wasn't using it any more. Blowing in it caused a duck sound, that familiar quack, quack. For some reason this was amazing.

As a kid, I wanted to speak the language of animals. As a kid, I made the natural connection, that what animals did was a language same as what we did. All you had to do was make the same sound and you could talk to a duck. It didn't dawn on me that ducks might communicate with each other but it wasn't the same as talk. Later I learned ducks did talk but without definitive words, about the same as the fans at a Packer game, who talk in explicative-rich bundles, flurried emotional bunches of noise. The same as people talk when caught in traffic jams, in zealous nondescriptive sounds not connected to regular brain function. As a language, this usually comes with lots of gestures.

It is a universal thing for a child to wish to speak to animals. Every kid starts out believing they can do this,

it's just a matter of learning the right sound, same as algebra. The participants don't really have to know what
it means, just respond with the right bundles of noise.
The plays of Shakespeare work something like this, as
does the Bible.

It wasn't that I wanted to discuss quantum physics
with bluejays, just say hello. Perhaps I had read too much
James Fenimore Cooper in whose *Last of the Mohicans*
Hawkeye and Uncas could talk to animals about simple
things like weather and good places to camp, but not
necessarily differential calculus.

My best friend was my next door neighbor, Tom Soik,
whose dad and sister had died in a car accident. He was
Polish and Catholic, as is a long ways different from being
Scots and Methodist, but still we talked. So I figured if
two varmints as wide apart as my friend Tom and I could
talk, we surely could talk to squirrels and bluejays. This
delusion was based on how different a Polish animal
could be from an Anglo-Saxon animal, and how different
were the Catholics in the days when I was a kid.

Since Tom had the same ambition, we devoted a major portion of our childhoods to learning to speak with
squirrels and muskrats. We'd go to the woods, he and I,
at every chance, to practice our skills of animal talk.

Squirrel talk was fairly easy and Uncle Jim's near
woods was a perfect squirrel woods. There were elms
there taller than God, with demigods of butternut and oak
in the fence line, the corn field was a little beyond. This
woods had all the prerequisites of a squirrel heaven. We'd
sit there, our backs against a tree and take turns convers-
ing with squirrels. What is required is a fat lump of spit
held behind the front teeth, and then to suck air past this
offending glob. The resulting sound is squirrel chatter
that you could amplify as needed, or repeat quickly as is
necessary to convey earnest emotion. The language we

learned was elemental, slanted to the emotive and the explicative; same as my older sister's language. Nothing intellectual or right-brained, just instinctive noise arbitrarily attached; like said, same as my sister.

When it came to animal languages, some were easy; cow talk was easy, so was horse talk. We never did get the bluejay vernacular down very good. No matter how hard we tried, the sound just didn't come out as bluejay. The crow, despite being next of kin to the bluejay, had an easy and well-equipped language, marked with all manner of shading and nuance. As a language, crow talk shared a lot with French, where the same word can mean goat, a sexual experience, a carpenter or a sawhorse. Crows did a similar thing, which was better by several orders of intellect than the language of my sister. Crow words could connote anger, curiosity, retreat, also hasty retreat, newly discovered food, watchfulness, hunger, owls, semi-dead food, pain, mind your own business, owl, red-tailed hawk, twenty-two caliber single shot, twenty-two caliber pump with a scope, and nearly-dead stuff. To the uninitiated the words might have sounded all the same, but taken in context, with syllabic variation, crows could have discussed theology and the quantum state without much difficulty. Tommy and I became sufficiently accomplished at crow talk that neither of us could shoot 'em, because we respected their brains.

Catbirds were similar to crows. Nothing can touch a catbird when it wants to play a variation on a theme by Hyden. Johann Sebastian Bach had nothing on catbirds. We spent the long summer evening in my mama's garden talking to catbirds. First we'd make a sound and the bird repeated it. Vowel for vowel. Phrase for phrase. Why that bird wasn't called the copy-catbird I don't know. It's relation in Tennessee is called the mockingbird, and, I suspect, for good reason.

When we were kids, sandhill cranes were rare, so it was natural to be hyper-attracted to the language of sandhills. They weren't anywhere as smart as crows or catbirds but they had a horn section the New York Philharmonic be ever so proud to own. Big-ass sound was the sandhill. Theirs was a Louie Armstrong sound, never mind Louie looked much more like an inflated prairie chicken. If ever there is a sound the equal of cosmic rays, the sandhill crane has it.

I liked the way sandhills defined the place, defined the shape and hollow of place with their language, a noise made for the emptiness and vista of marshes and prairies. How they filled that space, gave it defining vibration. You could hear a sandhill search a landscape same as an FBI agent frisks the pockets and pantlegs of a mobster. The noise goes through the pockets and billfolds of country, searches out where the cattails are, the tadpoles, turns the pockets of a place inside out. The sound takes on the shape of the land, same as a radar echo, 'cause it goes through grass different than trees. A sandhill crane was like a blind person reading braille, feeling the land with its call, what it was like and how it lies.

I came to think sandhill cranes were the same as the opera my grandfather listened to on Saturday afternoons. I don't think he understood opera any more than we understood sandhill cranes; it was just this chance to listen to some long-winded emotion, some jealous, some all-conquering noise.

We never did learn to talk with bluejays.

Screwed

M y father did not go to college, so he had neither a Bachelor of Science nor a Letter in Arts. He did not know who was Johann Sebastian Bach, neither Johann's musical wife nor his likable sons. Born was my father in a log house of a border precinct where he did perform and exhale those agricultural chores that have the profoundest probability of rendering a person to early dust.

A dairyman and tender of Holsteins, all of whom had names, his barn had one code of honor. Just one. This single commandment were we taught to follow with both our devotion and our faith. Do this one thing, obey this one command, and all would be well with us and with our universe, as happened to resemble a barn. Take my word for it, it was a universe.

What our father promised to his children of the barn was... follow this command and there shall be a green Christmas and a gravied Thanksgiving, there shall be cake and ice cream, and the good child shall inherit the domain in due and chosen time. This what our father said to us.

No Beatles
No Johnny Cash
Neither Beach Boys, no Elvis, no Little Jimmy Dick-

ens.

No jazz
No Rock & Roll
No Swing
Surely no Blues

Least not in the barn, not within the hearing of cows. No music that jangles, bangles or booms. This was his sacred word. Some music did, some did not; what the radio could and must by commandment play in the cow barn was music that did not... jangle. Did not bang or boom... did not excite the loins of the lower animals.

Music for the barn was that as did not roar or puff or swell. Did not raise an obnoxious babble with terrain as terrible as Afghanistan. For music to be worthy of cows it must speak gently and tend its airs reverently. Music that might speak well of Appalachia and of the prairie, whether of somewhere on the Ukraine or Iowa didn't matter. It could speak of the sea if it wished but avoid please the Straits of Magellan.

Our barn radio had, as did all well-rounded radios, two superlative and convenient knobs. I remember they were large knobs; not levers, not toggles, no bass control, no treble neither, just two knobs, large and simple knobs. One to do off and on, one to search the frequency. The knobs were bakelite or something like bakelite as was an artificial substance the like of plastic in an age that could still marvel at plastic. The frequency knob had a hole in it, a hole carefully enacted. Through it a screw was installed, counter-sunk, then painted over with window putty and boot polish so to give outward appearance of a tuning knob though quite incapable of tuning.

So it was our barn radio was frozen in frequency. The radio had full liberty to be turned on and off, and turned up loud, but to where tuned it offered no choice. Indelibly fixed was that radio, as is to say transfixed, to one source on the dial. One kind of noise, one kind of music. Mister Beethoven's music, Mr. Bach's music, Mozart too. Brahms, Sibelius, Mendelson if not necessarily Chopin who tended some say to jangle. This what my father did to the barn radio 50 years ago at the dawn of Rock and Roll. To protect his cows and honor lactation; no Blues, no Jazz, no Elvis. I thought at the time my father a particularly cruel man, illiterate to noises, out of spite I thought to whistle Rock and Roll. I failed, it cannot be done... whistle Rock and Roll. Whistle hymns and Sousa if you want, whistle lullabies and laments, but not Rock and Roll.

Music researchers Adrian North and Liam MacKenzie at the University of Leicester recently tested 1,000 Holsteins in two United Kingdom dairies. They exposed these milk cows to fast music, slow music and no music and they found out what my father already knew, sufficient to exacting the most corporal kind of punishment as can be visited on a radio. Screwing the knob to one band only, one station only, one kind of music only. What was once called long-hair music, suit-and-tie music, wine-and-crackers music; this we knew as milk music.

No Little Jimmy Dickens, no hot grease, no hog-calling music, if maybe a little chicken and gravy music. No music to cause or inspire jubilation of the feet or the heart. No jangles, nothing terrible, no music at all as might cause teenage boys to spin their tires and turn up the volume. What we heard was cow music, Holstein music, milking music, lactation and let-down music. This what my father knew so very well fifty years ago when the radio was AM only and the tuning knob was bakelite and screwed down tight.

Research now proves he was right. Cows give more milk when they listen to Beethoven's "Pastoral Symphony" as if they listen to Elvis' dog bark.

Too late came the research to better inform my father, it is tempo that is not kind to cows. One hundred beats per minute precisely is what milk cows need. Elvis and "Love Me Tender" might have mellowed our cows had the research been known, but our radio was screwed to Brahms and Dvorak, to Bach and Mozart, this for the sake of Holstein let-down. Three percent, the researchers say, three percent per day is the difference... six pounds, three quarts per cow, 273 gallons a year at $5 per hundredweight in 1952, $150 per cow, a new tractor every year because Beethoven did rule. Rock and Roll, as said, was screwed.

Cow Pie High

B axter Black, the former big animal veterinarian, reported that in third world countries children get high smelling cow pies. I can hear Baxter give that big cowboy laugh of his, how funny this all is ... getting high on cow pie ...

As a cow pie expert I am bothered Baxter Black did not give this cow pie high thing sober consideration, being Baxter is a role model for the community. Not that a big animal vet was the sort of person you want for a role model once you see what constitutes as a physical exam on a cow.

Back to this cow pie thing; it didn't surprise me that kids had finally discovered the cow pie high. The technique apparently is to insert one end of a soda straw into a fresh cow pie, put the other end into the nostril and inhale deeply. For those who want a more vivid experience, use two soda straws. Baxter did not detail the sort of high that results, whether a California type or a Colorado kind or some other type altogether.

I realize it may not be a major part of western literature, but there is such a thing as a cow pie high. Not that I ever tried the soda straw business but there were moments in my childhood when getting high on cow pie was routine though we personally favored the calf pud rather than the cow pie.

Calf pens in olden times were cleaned Saturday mornings, the chore done with a six-tine fork, this after the rest of the barn had been cleaned. That's what we called it then, cleaning barns. I realize now this was just another chemical dependency, cleaning barn was; an even worse addiction was the calf pen. It would take something on the order of an EPA air sampling device to know exactly what it was we were getting high on. Methane is the likely culprit, methane trapped in the alternating layers of calf pud and straw, that was released in volume by the six-tine fork, on the back end of the barn where the air didn't move and a kid sent to clean calf pens could get some serious levitation.

'Course we didn't know nothing about air quality back then, didn't know of the damage we were doing to our brains, or any good reason not to continue doing it. This whole business has of course broader cultural ramifications, as probably explains how kids end up becoming farmers in the first place, damaged brains and all. Kids who, if they had normal brain function, would not have become farmers.

I now realize it wasn't just the cow pie high that did us in. There were a whole bunch of drug addictions available: silo gas, hay gas, potato gas, oat bin gas, woodpile gas, cucumber patch gas. I also remember when trucks from the paper mills spread a strange smelling affluent on dirt roads and how we'd ride our bikes on those roads, before they softened up to plain old dirt again. The paper mill sludge glued the dirt together for awhile and we could touch some of that terminal velocity known to bicycles, which you ordinarily can't get close to on a dirt road. What the stuff was is anybody's guess. Other folks with all their brain cells intact might not have thought this nice, but they didn't suffer dirt roads in the first place.

As a kid I was high most of the time. If it wasn't cow pies it was sawing pine logs at Harold Edwards' woodlot mill. Even grown-ups got high doing this, so bug-eyed and toasted they'd end up working in their shirt sleeves in the middle of the winter. As any street cop knows, as soon as people start to shed clothes or go barefoot that is a pretty good indicator of chemical dependence.

Never was a place more brain-cell-deleterious than a calf pen on Saturday mornings at the far end of the barn. The modern workplace is now ventilated with so much fresh air a good chemical addiction isn't possible except to those who insist on running a chain saw indoors. Yup, we used to do that too, one of the great country highs was a chain saw. Used to start one in the outhouse just to get a good dose, same thing with the hot patch tire repair. Sometimes a bunch of us got together in the garage on Sunday afternoon while our dads were asleep and set off a tire patch without a tire in sight.

Myself I can still get off the ground a fair distance with a magic marker, fresh baked bread and spray can enamel. Fountain pens are good too, and cedar fence posts, and new erasers, and fresh baseballs ...

The Kite

The Liberty Corners School stood on the corner of County J and Double J, named after the flag mast as once reared up all sovereign like from the middle of the road. Nobody seems to remember how a mast complete with cross-trees and rigging came to be in the roadway. Every morning during the session a brace of older kids escorted the flag to the standard, fitted the grommets to the lanyard and hoisted Old Glory up the mast. The children in collect then recited the Pledge. Every morning.

The wind in the long glen between moraines did a peculiar thing with the flag; no sooner had it been half run up than the banner stood out taut as a jib sail. Never mind when the kids left home the wind according to the weather cock on the barn roof was northerly, somehow by the time they arrived at school it had steadied to a terse westerly heave, every day the same.

Eventually the blame for this meteorological abstraction was found in the design of the region where the auld heave, meaning the ice, exactly paralleled the new heave and the wind, no matter where it issues elsewhere, is detoured to the west after sliding over the back of the moraine.

This is the same manipulation as allows a canvas-driven vessel to tack an unseemly course into the nostril of the wind when every drop of natural credibility suggests the vessel ought be driven the other direction entire. Surprising it is to landlubbers to discover that ships actually flew more than they sailed.

Before gravel pits disemboweled the region, Liberty Corners was the richest farmland in the north end of the universe, comprised as it was of a friable loam accompanied by a dose of clay. As a result the school at Liberty Corners attracted the better grade of book-tender than could be afforded by school districts with less prosperous soil. The schoolmaster at the juncture of our story was one William Lightfoot, middle initial G for Gordon, his mother's maiden name. The year is 1927 and Master Lightfoot is enthralled like most of his countrymen by the daring aeronautical adventures attempted via primitive devices. The epitome of what then passed for science was to comprehend how an airplane wing worked. To this end Mr. Lightfoot decided the children would build kites and by fashioning these simple wings, understand the complex principles of lift.

When the school board heard the good teacher was allowing their children to make kites during school hours, they brought the master before their monthly tribunal for a dressing-down, as the then popular phrase put it. Referring as it did to shucking feathers off a beheaded chicken, the metaphor was applicable to what they intended to administer.

That they did not succeed was due to Mr. Lightfoot's contagious enthusiasm and his pointed inquiry whether they understood how the windmill in their very farmyard worked; how, exactly, horizontal force became circular. They having no idea kites, airplanes and windmills all succeeded by the same aerodynamic, a word they were to later proudly enunciate to their less knowledgable neighbors. As a result of the meeting, Mister Lightfoot was not reprimanded, in fact was given a generous bonus to his already lucrative salary of $37.50 per month plus commodities; a half bushel of apples in season, taters by the barrel, fresh ham, loaves of bread, and of course Miss Minnie's famous hand-dipped chocolates at Christmas.

The kite unit generated interest in the students for bigger and better things — the substantive question being how big was the largest kite ever and maybe they ought go for the world record and put Liberty Corners on the map same as Lindberg and Wiley Post. Being the consumate educator, Mr. Lightfoot sent the children to answer their own query, in the process of this basic research they engendered an enthusiasm he couldn't otherwise force on their resistant minds. Even the barn-scented farmboys were encouraged to dive into bottomless books and found it as refreshing as a secret dip in Uncle Charlie's fish pond. The answer to their question having several options, including the Wright Brothers' first attempt at Kitty Hawk, it being a kite. Also a conveyance in Scotland built by Percy Pilcher predating Kitty Hawk. There was an Icarus in the Bible, the patient schoolmaster correcting this forgivable observation, Icarus was Greek myth not Abrahamic.

The children of Liberty Corners were so enthralled by kites they felt compelled to further science and theorize what size kite is sufficient to lift a person. Eagerly they plunged into the dark arts of flight: the coefficient of lift and drag, the tetrahedinal of the classical wing versus a minor axis wing with flaps. The sum of this intelligence was, given a steady four-knot wind at Berry's knob, a lifting body of 112 foot square was required, with a sufficiently stout rope to hold it. Preferably attached to a tree.

Of this original research the school board was not appraised. In the fashion of all great explorers, the children recognized the science they were attempting was not meant for parents to know, they not being equipped to deal with aerodynamic principles, besides, would think it dangerous.

The student body of Liberty Corners fully expected some member of the class to die in the process, each eager to have the chance knowing the chalkboard thereafter'd have a brass plate in their honor. More notice than is given a farmkid killed by horse kick, influenza or polio.

The kite measured 32 foot long with a four foot cross-section, the fabric collected from stockings, various other garments and pajamas. The wing struts had formerly been fishing gear, cane poles to be precise. The bamboo split and bundled to make a wing cord, to whit the children learned the strength attributable to the Brooklyn bridge.

By ballot Fanny Trybitowski was elected to ride the kite for its trial flight on the first afternoon when the wind hit 14 knots. In the meantime, the kite was stored in the loft of the small horse barn behind the school, each student sworn by mutual consent to secrecy. Oscar Wentworth was chosen for the second flight.

The problem with kites as any kid can tell isn't the kite but the string. Once the string breaks the kite belongs to the ages, this exactly what befell Fanny T. As the craft began to rise from the ground, three of the young kids got over excited and let go the rope. Older kids responded instinctively with a swat at the stupid little kids with one hand and the cord slipped further in their other, the friction burning like a hot coal, they also let go.

So it happened that twenty-three seconds after Fanny T. became the first aviatrix of Liberty Corners, she also became the first freeflight casualty.

The released kite did as every wing is wont to in the

circumstance; it turned downwind, shedding lift as it did and plummeted approximately 56 feet to a new plowed field, breaking Fanny's arm and collarbone. She cried miserable because she hadn't been killed outright with a ceremonial burial and brass plaque, maybe even her picture at the head of the class along with George Washington.

The remains of the wing were promptly burned and together they rehearsed how Fanny was to tell her parents she had slipped on the school steps and fallen, but one of the younger kids blabbed. The next morning Mr. Lightfoot was seeking other employment.

Two years later Fanny died of diptheria, her classmates who attended the funeral all wished she had died scientifically instead. With a nameplate on the flag pole inscribed with the saving word "aviatrix." Where every morning the wind came over the moraine and in the long glen of Liberty Corners, stood out the stars and bars in a brave way.

Present at the Second Coming

My people were not the kind who put much store in the Second Coming. As a rule Methodists didn't, particularly Methodists of the Liberty Corners Buena Vista Methodee kirk. The Second Coming really was something of an immoral proposition, at least unseemly because it should have been done properly the first time. These the people who had built enough barns and cattle stalls to know that, knew if a thing was done right the first time it didn't need a second coming. Sure you can add a bulk milk tank or put in a pipeline but the same old and original barn stood the needs whether the farm had turned tractor or was still dead loyal to Percherons. Second Coming was for hooters, the noisy kind that get pried loose by a wandering evangelist who breaks womenfolk into a palsy and menfolk into sticky sweat. This was a discomforting line for religion to take, was leaning over-hard on the fence between decor and wanton noise. Man should keep his religion the same as he kept his barn, tight, quiet and maintained as cheaply as possible.

The Second Coming for my people came in the guise of the Acorn Machine Company newly arrived to the

village of Plover and the startling ware they were pro-
posing. The theory was a farmer could by the mere
throw of a switch exchange all the material the dairy
herd had deposited at their contrail for a new supply of
empty. The commercial sound of this business may not
sound all that promising to those unfamiliar, much less
the daily tending of the back end of a cow herd. The
simplest of hints of the sublimnity, of the splendor, of the
ecstasy available to the knowledgeable is conveyed by
the well-known proverb that an army succeeds, not on
the power of its will, patriotism or armament, but rather
the earnest feeding of its stomach. The cow has four of
the same appliances. Each one the size of a Maytag and
daily filled with a mixed ration of silage, ground feed
grain and hay in voluminous quantity. The result is a cow
spends a considerable portion of its lifetime exiting the
selfsame material. There is an impolite word here that is
however honest, honest about the nature of nature that is
seldom so equally honest. To call this effluent manure is
inaccurate. Manure is a French word, from the previous
word maneuver, referring to the distribution of the same
stuff on to the field. So the stuff isn't manure until it is
maneuvered, that is ever so obvious to those whose chore,
if not whose seeming task of life, is maneuver the business
from the backside of the cow to someplace else.

What the Acorn Machine Works of Plover had contrived was a system of links and paddles including an
inclined-plane. With the aid of this simple apparatus it
was possible to move cow manure out of the barn and
into the manure spreader with the ease of one electric
motor. The problem was no barn builder in all the previous centuries had imagined this development and hence
the barn wasn't designed for barn cleaners. Meaning the
Second Coming had arrived. The real Second Coming,
where the original version ain't' quite good enough.

A farmer who is loyal to the rural beatitudes is not easily persuaded to modernize, in other words alter his barn when it means he must do so with sledge hammer. With this instrument remove the concrete floor established in the barn at some real expense. Concrete, to those who don't know it personally, is a fairly permanent thing, it was meant to be. Removing it takes significant horsepower and the affability to breathe quantities of cement dust. When the agent for the Acorn Barn Cleaner Works told my father a mechanical marvel was his for only $525 plus freight he did not include the cost of removing the existing concrete floor.

Farmers there were in those times who did not buy barn cleaners and were thought by salesmen as backward, unmodern persons. These men had never removed cement. They did not know anything of the wage and pain experienced by the human frame from having to break out a concrete floor. Particularly one that had been installed on the belief that no Second Coming was necessary, much less likely. That good things were built to last and into which form the farmer had thrown every available metallic trash, fence wire and crib cage, barbell, digger link that he and several obliging neighbors possessed. The result was a permanent sort of concrete able to cap the wrath of any volcano, to last until the sun grew old and would in due course melt the entire earth except for a few orbiting rectangles of barn floors. Made to last, stout as the New Testament itself and equally as eternal.

As said, the Testament of barns had not figured on barn cleaners doing the most odious of farm chores and at the mere flick of a switch. It might have been different if no one broke the ancient honor, and none purchased the newfangled holy-cow wonder as is a barn cleaner. But let one farmer in any neighborhood buy a barn cleaner and brave the terrible days spent breaking concrete, and all of them were simultaneously doomed. If one of their kind was seen going down the town road on his way to manuring, seen in clothes that had on them not the slightest particle of miscue. Clean and fresh as on a Sunday morning and the rest of them besplattrered and brownly wet, then the rest of them were compelled by a greater force than Einstein can reckon to do the same.

So in the course of eons, or as farmers know time, the Second Coming did arrive. Barns were reborn with an effort equal to that as was required to build them in the first place. Floors as solid as Gibraltar were hammered into grey dust and new floors poured with roller wheels in the corners and bridges at the alleyways and a great derrick of creosoted wood angling from the barn's far quarter that so gracefully slid the consuming ooze of the herd into a waiting manure spreader. Then this farmer too could join the great clean chorus of the exultant few who plied the township roads clean as the angels themselves in their overalls. Something ought have told them it wouldn't last.

The reason it didn't occur to farmers this couldn't last is logical enough if any had presumed to think about it. Cow manure as the standard legal tender of a country life is a pretty affable product during the spring, summer and fall. When properly strawed this barn mix was a quite cheerful milieu, almost a delight to work with. During winter it is something else. What was a charitable, even warm product in the barn during the summer is now a frozen rock of cow doo. It froze on the chain, it froze on the hubs, it made a mockery of the driving gears. The odd chunk caught, the motor whined and all that mechanical energy in that cast iron chain contracted and contracted until the barn itself sensed the tension and was about to explode itself into a zillion smithereens when, happily, the chain broke. A dull thud of a sound it was. Some link somewhere in all that mire of cow poop was broken and now it was for the farmer, or his child, to find by fork, by shovel and by god. Search out on hands and knees feeling your way along each link until the broken one was found, and then with hand, elbows and clinched teeth retrieve the slack, align the chain and install a new link. It was not a pretty business. It was not spotless. In true fact it was a great deal worse than cleaning the barn by hand. One episode of this was enough to make one wonder whether it was better the way previous. That maybe the fork wasn't so bad. Neither was the wheelbarrow so ignominious as was this demeaning search on hands and knees fingering every forkful until the sad broken link was found.

There were farmers in our township who junked their barn cleaners and went back to the original fork. Others learned to live in a state of perpetual anxiety and as a result of this caution worked the business end of the loader with a fork to clean every link and slide lest it freeze. The scene of this in winter, when it is cold outside and the wind blows hard and quite a few objects are airborne. To land, the odds unequal here, down the neck or in the ear of the attendant. Which led farmers to wonder about those great theological themes. Whether the original wasn't good enough and if so, why was the Second Coming so gosh darn popular? Knowing, as did all the apostles, that the price of modernization is anxiety, that what is now so nifty and modern might break. And what happened then might well have curled the toes of the most primitive savage.

There is to every farmkid a certain intimacy with nature and nature's god. It comes at odd moments. The capacity to see what prophets and mystics can not. That for every new gadget, every new gizmo, every labor-sav-

ing appliance and accessory is a new price. Like as not a
new humiliation, that you will, when the chain breaks be
worse off than what you thought to improve. The only
option was to make your peace with the maneuvers of the
world and know in the end, it's the same old manure.

Negotiations on Desire

My wife tells me I am a catalog nut, which isn't true. My pleasure in catalogs is only the relish of research, honest! To my thinking catalogs are the best kind of indicator you could ever hope to examine culture, if you want to find out of what dream elements a culture is made, read through its catalogs. The wealth is here to see, the extravagance, the decoration, the silliness, the dreams, the faith, the patriotic — all viewable in catalogs, and you can't catch a disease from a catalog. Forget the Dow Jones averages, forget *Washington Post* surveys; instead look through the catalogs.

It is true I receive catalogs and multiples of catalogs, in particular Christmas catalogs. When this is not enough, I send for others. The woman of me complains that catalogs don't burn and produce various heavy metal toxins if they do. I reply with the well known Platonic, "know thy catalog and so know thyself." That I am this way is the result of my sand farm metamorphosis when a big league purchase in the time of my youth was a dime tube of Daisy brand Bullseye BB's. Otherwise, what all else I desired or wished, what I yearned for and plundered after in my heart existed in pictorial form only. After some slight adjustments I found this to be all I honestly needed of the consumer society. Were I desirous of a Swiss Army knife, the kind with the knife, fork, spoon, a compass on jewel bearings, scissors, water-proof matches, signal mirror and magnifying glass with which I could save my life if Stalin ever took over the township, all I had to do to have that knife was cut out the picture and pin it to the knotty pine wallpaper of my bedroom wall. That was it. I owned in all but the most trifling aspects, a genuine Swiss Army knife. With the early dawn the light came in the window and shone on the knife, causing it to hover there on the wall in solid rendition. Almost real. Almost there, that red Swiss Army, almost, on my wall. From the floor I heard the rousals of my waking father. The click of the bed light. The sound of suspense of Pa's feet swinging to the edge of the bed and falling after a long moment to the floor. From the sounds I know before anything else he put on his socks. I've never seen him actually dress himself but I knew the order exactly. First he skinned into his long-johns, wiggling his knees, adjusting the hang of the seat, then like a knight at the tournaments he stepped into the stays of his battle armor, that quintessential exoskeleton of bib overalls. They jingled as he moved into them. Among the earth's unacknowledged beauties is that joyous sound of brass button bibs ringing in the otherwise ruined landscape of early morning. The noise less of the calling of temple bells and the invitation to prayer as the sound of harness, of the draft animal being dressed well and lovingly for another day's pull. Of my father I believed he needed bib overalls as a specific ingredient to get him upright, to get him stood up against the new farm morning. I listened as he went to the refrigerator for a long drink of milk. From the water glass on the kitchen table he retrieved his teeth. For some reason they clicked as he installed them.

Behind the screen at the back door he lifted his denim Saxon from its peg, it too sang with buttons, then his hat from the shelf, and in final Beethoven notes he stomped his feet into a pair of thick farm rubbers.

From the corner bedchamber in that white farmhouse I listened as he crossed the yard, the squeak of the barn door opening, the snap of the light switches, then another minor chord as the door closed. Pa had tried to affix the self-closer hardware from the hardware store to that door. They tended to slam-dunk a door when a person wasn't in the mood for slam-dunk. What the door had was his own invention; a screw eye, a pulley, a piece of clothes-line and a battered remnant of worm gear for weight. Pa tried five weights before he found the exact right pace. A hunk of junk that brought the door closed with both the surety he wanted yet avoiding the acrimony that'd foul a morning with too much abruptness.

As I listened to my father set up the milking I'd look up at my Swiss Army knife. In the soft folds of first light you couldn't tell it was only a picture. I had then the thorough satisfaction that Swiss Army knife really belonged to me and was only sitting on a shelf. The more I looked at it the more it was real. I looked at it and thought how it would feel in my pocket, important and heavy as a loaded six-gun. That good and that heavy is a Swiss Army. I thought about pushing the silage cart with that Swiss Army knife in my pocket. And dumping shotgun cans and throwing down silage and hay and playing basketball, in the barn. Basketball as we played basketball in a ten-degree haymow. I knew then in a slow sinking realization that the Swiss Army knife I had on my bedroom wall wouldn't do at all. Even if the Russian's invaded, it wasn't worth the burden of 1 3/4 pounds of knife in my pocket. The knife with the ten blades and a hook ladder with a hydraulic cylinder, a knife I knew could not benefit me because it was... too much. Too heavy, too big in the pocket, too much to choose from; besides, the blades, all those blades would probably rust up and be in the end, just when I needed them, frozen in their slots. What I really wanted was the feedmill knife, two blades only and not too good to lose.

After a while I took the picture of the Swiss Army knife off my wall and put it in the waste basket Mama used to start the stove fire in the morning, the stove I heard her rattle while Pa was taking the surcingles off their pegs over the nine light barn window.

Catalogs have served me in my career as a farmboy, taught me the purpose of possession without the bother of possession. The same as I came to know my father and his habits without actually seeing them. My tin-plated 75-cent hardware jackknife did just fine and when I lost it, a period of mourning was not required. I had learned I never really wanted a Swiss Army knife, with its four blades, a knife, a fork and the spoon. Besides, you couldn't play haymow basketball with the one-and-a half-pound Swiss Army in your pocket.

FarmKid Winter:
Remembering Snow

I remember the winter better than I remember the summer. I remember once we chiseled the geese out of their watering pans in the morning. They being a superior order of animals spent the afternoon in the water trough and one fierce night it and they froze solid. Chiseled them out one at a time with a wood chisel and mallet. The geese, the superior creatures they were, none the worse for it.

When I was a farmkid we always postponed "getting up wood" until winter was dead earnest, in the meantime burning every windfall and loose board to warm that monster and hollow farmhouse. The reason we were so late to the woods was we had just finished those multiple "last chores;" picking corn, spreading lime, grading potatoes. Stovewood always came last since it was only our comfort that mattered, not the cows, the chickens or field pH.

Some folks turn romantic when they think of wood fires, with its fresh paint essence of pine, the heady, mushroomy smolder of oak. Myself, I took maximum pleasure in tires, old tires, burning old tires. They the only thing as rendered the arctic woods of our last farm chore the least length of cheerful. First we heaped a brush pile higher than a straw rick, then beneath it slid half a dozen threadbare tires, doused the condemned with motor oil, a bit of raw gasoline for a fuse, and tossed in the match. Instant conflagration. I knew then it wasn't the witches the Inquisition was after so much as the marvel of their combustion. Half volcano, half funeral pyre. Our fire smelled like you'd expect a burning corpse to smell, sticky, glue-faced smoke whose vise-grip stench clamped onto your clothes and won't let go. If not exactly scenic, this fire did banish cold anywhere within the radius of fifty yards, in this circle was full-tilt summer. We couldn't hardly get close enough to refuel it before the skin melted off our bones. We worked then in a narrow twilight between too cold and too blame hot, down to our shirtsleeves on a day no kinder than 12° at high noon. Gleeful in this fragile tropic, happy to be at work bare-handed without mittens, mufflers or overshoes. Hell, we believed, was a similar heck, fueled also by demonic tires. At least that was our simple theology, if farmkids can be said to have a theology. Hell was just a large version of our swamp fire and if you were smart there, too, you learned to work the temperate zone between where melts the skin and where the ice is not yet thawed. Just so we, mere children, fell in love and league with winter, by this fire and by our effort rendered comfortable. It was one of those life lessons, how with match and a brush pile even the obviously inhospitable can be rendered most decorous. Winter for a person of such a wisdom is never again the sordid imposition of rotten climatology, instead an excuse to invent the means to comfort, the challenge to be that phenomenon, of the comfortable despite the circumstance.

Some farmers when they get rancid, go south, openly admitting they are too old for winter. I would miss the desolation of which snow is capable, only war and plague can do for countryside what snow does. Six inches will do but it must be hammer-driven, seven or eight is better. A foot is to my mind truly superlative, the wind tamping it down like cannon powder. In the instant the modern age drops away and in its place it is the 18th Century again, maybe the 17th, a premium grade stillness reigns. The snow, the wind absorb all else. Every place is now newly distant from every other, lost in this virgin worshipful silence. Each farmhouse isolated, swinging into the dark on an orbit to itself.

Once when I was a kid it snowed three days straight without pity or let-up. Didn't matter to us, Mama had the cellar, with ample head-high shelves filled to everlasting, capable of re-supply to the Army of the Potomac. With the road closed off we put the accumulating milk in spare cans kept for just such event, when they filled we sought out washtubs, copper boilers, mop pails, laundry tubs. There would have been milk in galoshes and the canoe had the storm not slackened off.

Another time the wind fashioned a snowdrift clean up the flank of the stave silo. Wasn't the tallest silo in the world, still, that was one impressive snowdrift. The Guggenheim might have taken it for display had we figured how to preserve it. Nearly killed Mama when we discovered the penchant that drift had for acceleration. Using nothing more than a scrap of metal roofing, the end curled over our galoshes, we hunkered down while a brother kick-started the bombardment. By our estimate we hit 200 mph, being that silo was near forty feet high and so too the drift. Besides, I had the pedal to the metal. When snow is that cold there ain't any friction and I coasted a mile out across widow Soik's field, almost I think to warp speed. Walking back was a problem.

Big snow meant caves, caves and snow forts and castles and catacombs and watch towers and labyrinths.

Every town road had in their snow banks its own version
of the Sierra Nevada, parallel mountain chains courtesy of
the town plow. Here a kid with a sawed-off shovel could
dig mines, burrows, warrens, dungeons, cellars, kivas,
an entire civilization under the snowbank. I don't know
why this so appealed to me, the thought of an alternative civilization, a place where pirates and Indians and
the clans could still be safe. So could horses and wolves
and lots of other creatures that regular civilization thinks
disrespectful. We had dens carved out in the snowbank,
with fireplaces and chimneys where we smoked our
cherished collection of cigarette butts. The hallways were
carpeted with potato sacks. We had ventilation shafts
and lookout towers. If we hadn't had to spend every
Saturday in the woods and half the Sabbath in church,
we coulda provoked a colossal architecture, equal I think
to the Empire of the Nile, least till thaw ruined it.

Mama worried some about us getting crushed in our
caves by the town plow if they had the wing out. She
knew from experience the heck this performed on a mailbox. She ought not have worried. Remarkable to think
how well you can hear the plow when you're buried in
the medium. Besides, Oscar Whipple who drove the big
Oshkosh, got paid by the hour and some winters being
lean he had to take advantage while the snow was deep.
Can't do a job on snow banks at much over 16 mph and
still miss the mailboxes. The one time the town chairman
made the mistake of questioning the number of hours on
his time card, the next week there were more mailboxes
lying dead in the road than you could shake a stick at.
Besides, Oscar being a farmkid himself knew the sign of
the snow bank entrance hole, a flap door made of a potato sack and from the nearby flag pole, the declaratory
ensign of white underwear. A strange flag compared
to the routine signal buntings of the rest of the world's

nations. But then this was the other kind, the farmkid civilization.

I have decided when I am old I shall sit in a chair by a winter window, my feet on a stool, afghan across my shoulders. Snow you see is the cousin of Buddhism. Snow like hymn singing can settle your mind better than most other patent cures. Snow is falling somewhere always, in that I am comforted, especially with the woodpile well done. I shall contemplate there. Not on the Torah, not on the prophets or the profits, not on philosophers but on snow. I shall remember snow.

FarmKid Winter: Icicle

News reports during the late winter advise people to be careful of ice, those long, dangerous icicles that form in roof valleys, some growing in size to be quite enormous. A man was killed in Beloit when an icicle collapsed upon him. Another caused a fire when it ruptured a gas meter.

The farmhouse of my youth followed a logical pattern of agrarian progress, at least we thought it was logical. What started out as a house of one design became after several moltings and evolutions something else, which is to say added to. Every so often the house morphed, shed its skin and transformed. A bit like an insect was our farmhouse, if an architect might suggest perhaps it was the butterfly changing into the worm. The first trespass as the addition of a summer kitchen, then the wood shed became a garage, a bay window arrived. Roof was added to roof, gables came and went; shed roof and lean-to, mansard and hip; quite a jumble it all was of roof meet and drainage, none of which seemed to matter. Except during the balmy soft ends of winter when vigorous sun and tilted drainage diverted all this melt toward one common spill. Was here the cross-connects and accidentals of my father's and grandfather's house additions came to consequence. Thus empowered, the roofs conspired and formed ices of such proportions and vehemence we the childs of that house could not help but joyously worship them. There were icicles the size of trees; so maybe they were only saplings but still they were trees and evidently well rooted to the roof of the house. It was these trees as inspired us to imagine what might grow from the house roof if a bit more snow was added, that a rising winter sun could on the next bright day convert to purest ice.

It is not a rare thing for children to love snow. If left to themselves children will acclimatize to that substance and soon have caves and igloos made. Some would spend the entire winter there if their parents had but similar adventure. Neither is it a rare thing for children to carry snow great and incredible distances if something more can be made of it. It was while our parents weren't looking, which on the farm happily is most of the time, that we did via a 2 x 4 ladder carry buckets of snow to the roof of the house, and add this to the burden already present. Our father, distracted, paid no attention. In between chores we added more snow. A daily devotion it was, from the back side of the house, using that 2 x 4 ladder, to add more snow. Bucket followed bucket, filled and thrown over and raked smooth to look natural despite it hadn't snowed for two weeks. Our father was, as is the nature of fathers, entirely occupied by the cost of living, the mysterious death of calves, the onset of mastitis, and the daily battle with the hand crank on the Allis Chalmers tractor. He did not notice the roof never completely melted of snow. Nor did he notice the sapling oak of an icicle on the front porch was now several hundred board feet more than a sapling.

We continued to ferry more snow, bucket by bucket, ice chunks themselves if they were to be had for there was more water in ice than in snow, this we knew because

the bucket was heavier. The thought passed our mind
that a garden hose might speed this, but it was frozen
solid and the spigot turned off in the cellar. Besides, he
might catch on.

By the time we finally decided one day in March to
end this adventure, the farmhouse had before it four
colonnades just like Mt. Vernon. Not columns of lath
and plaster, not of mortar and grout but of perfect, jewel-
like ice. Ice big around as a beer barrel with a delicately
rippled surface ever so much better than Grecian columns
seen befronting antebellum mansions. We were fittingly
proud of our achievement, a new agrarian architecture
this surely was and we three farmboys were responsible
and ever after credited in the manuals and digests of
house design as the originators of the ice-pillar look.
Ever so much better than Frank Lloyd Wright; and talk
about using natural earth elements, the prairie-style had
nothing on the "glacial look." How to convert this to a
construction technique we did not know. Glass perhaps,
molten insulators, or perhaps more simply a large size
mason jar complete with carrots, stewed tomatoes and
chicken feet... installed as columns before farmhouses
as wanted the latest in architectural style. Harking not
only to the godly nature of ice and winter and a good
seamless metal roof but the favors granted to deserving
humanity by the mason jar.

The laurels due three farmboys in the architectural
journals never took place for a sudden over-bitten thaw
occurred and those ices fell from the roof. The first with
such seismic repercussion it scared our mother to a point
of panic, that the others would cave inward and smash
the porch entirely. To quiet her fears our father hitched a
rope and chain to the surviving columns and pulled them
off the house, along with the rain gutter. It dawned then
on our parents that these ices were not entirely native.

Before the ladder and bucket could be fingerprinted by the FBI we confessed. As was the pattern, the younger brother fessed up first, which obligated an even greater confession from the elder brother including a solution to crimes quite distant from the ice architecture.

I remain yet an admirer of ices, of ices hanging and ices precarious, of ice as the perfect abstraction, the like that Picasso might do if infected with rabies. I think it is a wilderness look, when a house grows fabulous fangs. An elementary worship of winter. A dedication to the innate character of the northern latitudes whose climate builds character and grit. So what if they kill a bystander or two, art this good is still worth the price. The Himalayas do this all the time and nobody seems to mind. Besides, there is a certain crude pleasure of being a native of such a distant, far-removed place as seasonally remakes a farmhouse, into a Grecian temple.

FarmKid Winter:
The Town Plow

T he official hierarchy in the township commences with the town chairman, whose appointment is by God; thence follow the supervisors, close on is the assessor. Less close is the dog catcher who, if he is good at his work, is a character the Humane Society would not approve. The constable is an honorary office because the sheriff's department doesn't want just anybody to have arrest power. At the bottom of this chain of command is the town clerk, who like as not is the only person who knows what is going on in the township, and how to get it going if it ain't.

The unofficial hierarchy of the township begins elsewhere, wherein the commander-in-chief is none other than the number one driver of the number one town plow. In the unabridged history of snow, there has never been a sovereign throne the equal of that mortal person established to rule with the town's number one Oshkosh. For those who do not know what is an Oshkosh, describing it as a truck is of no help. Were a weapon's engineer to combine the best attributes of one ore boat, one Sherman tank, one submarine, one drawbridge and one Parisian salon, the result be an Oshkosh snow plow. A truck that can proceed anywhere in middling comfort, whether 20,000 leagues under the snow, or smashing through the coral reef left by 30 mph winds and hard packed for two days straight.

Before leather seats became popular in luxury cars, Oshkosh snowplows had them. The legend is the seats were more than leather, in fact genuine grizzly bear hide tanned and heat-formed to exactly fit the hind end of the plow driver. It was more a saddle than a seat, lacking only the saddle horn. Before seat belts bear hide was the only way a snowplow driver stayed put; by a little known chemical process, the damp of his pants welded him in place same as a seat belt but with none of the bother.

Oscar Whipple piloted the town's number one plow, for forty years he drove the town's jewel and not about to trade places with Mark Antony the night he took Cleopatra under the quilt. Driving an Oshkosh through six inches of new fallen was an imperial sensation. Was like being in second command of God. Was an Oshkosh.

The Oshkosh came from the factory with the governor pre-set at 58 mph. Took an odd and small wrench to adjust it otherwise, this sent via registered mail to the town chairman. Being for a responsible elected official to decide whether to leave the governor be and throw away that wrench or give it over to the number one driver of the number one truck. Snow plowing, it needs be understood, didn't pay that well, meaning the town couldn't get college graduates to do it, few farmers either. If the town wanted a driver to stay on it had to provide dispensation. In Oscar Whipple's case it was that odd small wrench.

Commendable enough snow plowing is accomplished at 58 miles per hour, just like the pre-set governor said. Great snow plowing requires 70 mph, the Oshkosh capable enough up to about six inches, after which even the Oshkosh suffered. Of importance was to have the blade done up premium, buffed and waxed with the best carnauba from the Amazon. The result looked more like a telescope reflector than a town plow. Had a certain menacing look, like a device as could wound winter if it had to. There is a law of physics that requires 70 mph for optimum snowplowing, which law exactly doesn't matter. Any less than 70 and the six inches of new fallen just flops over like a sodden mattress, ending up next to the road, in turn causing the road to drift closed in the next half hour if the wind is up. At 70 mph Oscar Whipple could throw snow forty rods over, keep the road open a couple hours more and have a paying spectacle besides.

In olden times cop cars had red flashing lights and there were plenty of kids who wished to become cops for the sake of those snazzy lights. The same career aspirations were inoculated by the bright paint and gleaming fixtures of the fire engine. In our town farmkids wanted to grow up and take over the number one plow. While a cop car is a spectacle, that snow plow was more; it was an oracle disguised as a carnival; it was a behemoth; it was semi-divine; it was awesome with the blue strobe lights on the cabin roof, marker lights on the blade, twin blue rows along the flank of the vehicle and two frost-covered specters at the tail end. On a still winter night with all those lights on and a contrail languishing out behind, a strategic bomber couldn't match that plow truck. Any kid who saw knew it was the pinnacle of human experience and so ordered his life so he too could pilot the Number One town Oshkosh.

In the distance we heard it. The Oshkosh sorta grunted, like a pig does, not an admirable noise perhaps but an honest one. As it came closer the cupboard commenced to rattle, closer yet a tumultuous near-earthquake quality rumble. If it weren't for the over-mantle of snow quenching that sound, the seismic waves of the Number One plow would shake window panes loose of their brittle putty. At the head of the road we watched Oscar setting up his run. The heater fan turned up full to keep the windshield thawed, his hat on backwards, Oscar gauging the road. Aim counted to snowplowing 'cause once up a terminal velocity, steering the Oshkosh wasn't so practicable as was sorta sailing it. A good driver had to have a natural trigonometry in them to do the town road without clipping off every mailbox and debarking every tree and lilac as had residence there.

Night was the best time for snow plowing. No cars in the way. No tractors. No kids on sleds. No one to see what happened exactly to their mailbox.. Oscar was a night kind anyhow owing as he ran 'coon dogs for enlightenment. The wind quits about sundown if its gonna and the roads empty so the plow doesn't have to dodge manure spreaders and milk trucks. Set the Oshkosh straight, nudge the edge of the blade against the snow bank, turn the wheel a bit to starboard and all there is left to do is weld the throttle down. Was the snout of the truck turned into the snow bank as held the truck straight, steering wheel had nothing to do with it. At 70 mph Oscar took his hands off the wheel and went barreling down the road as if on remote control, eating doughnuts with one hand, a coffee mug in the other. Unless he hit a buried mailbox or something, which didn't cause any harm only to send the truck to the opposite bank. Oscar didn't often get off course, knew every mailbox and oak stump in the township. The part-time drivers in the number two truck tried what Oscar did and we'd see the plow careening back and forth between the snow banks rattling up the guts of anybody inside. After a dose of twisted bowel and neck dislocation, most quit trying to do an Oscar without an Oshkosh.

In the wake of Oscar's Number One hung this plume of mystified snow. Crazy thing is, the job of the town plow was to move snow, shove it aside which it did; but there was a part, a portion of the snow that wasn't just shoved out of the way. It was etherized. Rendered into particles so minute, so elementary they just hung in natural suspension to the weight of a dark winter night. Hung there, tinkling, a faint ethereal tinkling, morphed into some rare substance by the passing of Oscar's Number One. This ghostly specter would hang in the atmosphere long after the truck passed, kicked by that polished blade into sublime elementariness. The township never looked a braver place than what it did in the wake of the Oshkosh. The blue light flashing its wizarding effect, the pulse of the truck felt through our feet. The infinitesimal snow as it settled spent a krinkling muse, as someone sweeping up the finely broken glass of champagne flutes.

I remember those winter nights, my face half frozen to the pane, watching, waiting for Oscar. His blue lights coursing the next town road over, then another, each pass marked by that fluorescent tail. I wanted nothing more than to become an economic failure, even have a drinking problem if I must, so I too might drive that town plow. If in other places Picasso and Einstein mattered and what Georgia O'Keefe drew was a marvel, out that winter window in an epoch of lonely roads, Oscar Whipple was an artist. Only his wasn't sissy stuff with a paint brush or a marble hammer... his was by Oshkosh and six inches of new fallen.

FarmKid Winter:
History of a Snowball

Oscar Whipple was a demigod in our township same as John Thomas who broke the seven-foot barrier in the high jump, same as Roger Bannister who bit off the wire surrounding the four-minute mile, same as Dexter Eckles who climbed the north face of Al Poltier's blue Harvestor without the aid of gear, oxygen or Sherpas.

Oscar piloted the town plow, a four-wheel drive Oshkosh that possessed the same aura as a Grand Prix Ferrari, least to farmkids it did. Capable it was of 70 mph with three ton of salt/sand mix in the bunk and a ton and a half of wrought-iron hanging off the front end. Not to forget the wing on the starboard quarter, complete with six ebony-knobbed levers, a hydraulic cylinder the size of a road culvert, heavy duty windshield wipers, a 720 cubic inch diesel, 18-speed gear-box, three-speed differential, air brakes, 36 amps worth of marker lights, the non-regulation open exhaust of a certified emergency vehicle, and seats upholstered in real leather. Every kid in our township knew it was grizzly bear hide reserved by presidential proclamation for Oshkosh snowplows even if it meant the extirpation of the grizzly to get it.

Oscar Whipple's virtuosity with the Oshkosh was well-known throughout the township. The man never met a drift he couldn't vanquish, not even that horrid and occasionally demonic road on the west flank of the moraine. A road whose entire length is canopied with black locust, dense as lilacs but taller by twice, whose effect is to condense every loose flake inside the arch of those same trees and stop up the road tighter than a convention hall toilet.

For a generation the town chairman badgered the farmer to remove those locusts, this to forestall snow drifts hard as pig iron and about as heavy. The farmer's reluctance was due to the refreshment of that road about mid-May when the blossoms came forth. A simple town road as seemed now urgently visited by the gods and demigods; a throne hall of their kind for the pea-petalled locust blossoms fell on every passing tractor and asparagus hunter like the sincerest blessing of the cosmos. In the end it didn't matter, Oscar and the Oshkosh put in an extra half-day to keep that road from drifting tight in the first place, 'cepting the time Oscar's Great Aunt Mildred died at Bevent, the wake coinciding with one of those dead-eye westerlies at gale force six scouring up every loose snowflake from six townships, tumbling this trash till it reached the moraine road and those locusts. Eight foot drifts harder than uranium bullets. Oscar being pall bearer at the funeral couldn't just declare his snow authority and leave; anyhow, nobody lives on the moraine road. Still, a township as thinks itself up to snuff can't suffer a clogged arterial; besides, it was the shortcut to the Somer's tater shed who serves hot French fries Saturday afternoon with beer and pinochle over by the shop stove.

Oscar's method of extreme eradication was to detach the outside mirrors, cover over the marker lights with duct tape and hit the drift with the V-blade set up narrow.

This done as fast as possible. When the drift stopped his forward progress, he backed up the truck a quarter mile and reapplied the ointment. Hitting the drift at 60 per with tire chains and open exhaust, not to mention 10 tons of Oshkosh. The principle exactly comparable to the use of a splitting wedge and sledge hammer. By and by Oscar and the Oshkosh emerged from the other end of the moraine road and the township was safe and could feel modern again.

Once upon a time my brother, widow Soik's son and I started a snowball. Originally we intended a snowman but got intoxicated from rolling that snowball. This how it is when the snow is just exactly precisely absolute, perfectly right snowball-rolling snow. This right doesn't happen but once in a millennium. We rolled the snowball far as we could till it stood most of six foot in diameter, we were aided by the slight downgrade of the road so we didn't have to roll it entirely our ownselves, just tip it some, this way and that so it rolled even. The snowball stopped, as farmboy bad luck would have it, dab smuck in the middle of the road. The day was rapidly going on dark and now the road with this monster snowball in the traffic lane, right in the middle where every country person drives. Six foot in diameter. Half gravel, half ice, half dead cat, half snow. How it blended with the snow. A head-on collision with this asteroid was gonna kill somebody. Wisely, we fled the scene.

My younger brother immediately ratted, telling Pa about the enormous snowball we made and how it like to kill somebody, probably had already, and being the first to confess he wasn't going to serve the prison term. As you can probably guess, my kid brother ended up going to law school. Pa laughed, saying it didn't matter. Patted him on the head 'cause he was little even for a farmkid. When Pa saw the look in my eyes he got worried, thinking maybe he better have a look at this "snowball." Two minutes later he came running in, his pantlegs flying like when the heifers are out, telling Mama to call the town garage to send Oscar and how he should damn sight hurry.

Ten minutes later we heard the snort of the Oshkosh, Pa having already put the Allis Chalmers tractor cross-ways of the road like he'd seen done on Dragnet. We climbed on the snow bank to watch Oscar hit the snowball at 70 mph and bust it back to the radioactive particles. Least that is what we expected. Instead Oscar nudged the mammoth blade of the Number One plow against the snowball. We thought he was marking the spot where he was to slug it same as a body does splitting wood. Instead, he commenced rolling it, butting it this way, then that. The snow as I said perfect snow. When that snowball got rolling crooked, Oscar butted it right with the Oshkosh. By the time it rolled in our yard it stood thirty feet high. Honest. I say it was only thirty when it coulda been a hundred feet and then only stretching a little. The biggest gawd darn snowball you ever want to see. Took three eyes to see the entire thing. It weighed right up there with Pluto, a planet it was almost, sitting in our yard.

Was half past July before it melted, which is saying a lot standing as it did out in the perpendicular sun. Though the dirt, gravel and dead cats are known to slow the thaw. How it squatted on a warm afternoon, sighing almost, wishing it'd been born in outer space where it mighta lived a million zillion years orbiting with Halley's, safe out there in the cold dark of that outer winter.

We never did a snowball like that again. Wasn't ever again the exactly right kind of snow. And 'cause it'd taken three kids to try and Widow Soik had moved to the village. Besides, maybe next time Oscar'd just smack it. Made a kid, even a dumb farmkid, think about genesis and God and rolling snowballs and how it ain't enough for just one thing to be in the mood. Snow's gotta be right and the Oshkosh available and your best friend can't go moving to the village. And how very unlikely ordinary things are, whether the planets or anything else. Never mind what might happen if the wrong sort, I mean humorless, collided with it before you got your planet out of the road. Which is why only the gods are gods and them only if they pilot an Oshkosh.

Mailbox Hockey

The original purpose of the farm-size mailbox was to shelter those things farmers received via U.S. Post. The age is known to farm historians as the Mail Order Generation, also known as the Pre-Fleet Farm Epoch. The mailbox in this special interlude was the central entertainment in farm life; everything that mattered came by way of it. As a communication device it was sorta like a television antenna except television antennas can't differentiate between farm and non-farm forms of life like a mailbox. Folks with small mailboxes did not receive the General Winter and Summer Catalog from the Emporiums of Merchandise, they did not buy shoes and teapots by mail. People with small mailboxes did not have a need for that mail shed at the end of the lane. They did not have baby chicks coming, neither saw blades, window curtains, coil springs or Betty Crocker cutlery delivered one utensil at a time. This probably why people with small mailboxes didn't thrive in the farmship. They always figured they needed somewhere else to survive. What they needed was a big mailbox and catalogs enough to go with it.

A mailbox alone on the farm road is more than alone, it is more than vulnerable, it is an invitation to sport. A big farm mailbox has a taunting look, especially alone at night and its you and the guys with the windows down and a baseball bat. The scene then is 27 mph, a bat, a mailbox and a kid, a kid with a crew-cut projecting three-quarters of his torso out the back window. Unknown to the kid are the pole barn nails affixing the mailbox to the post. The post is white oak. Set in cement. Ten feet in the ground. Five cubic yards of cement. It is less the kid striking at the mailbox as the reverse. The impact neatly catapults him from the car, saved only from dismemberment by his knobby knees. The rebound of the bat does a number on the back window of the car. Like I said, this was a sport once, though the odds were in favor the mailbox.

Sport did not return until someone discovered, probably the kid with the dislocated shoulder and an enduring grudge, now working on the town crew, that the length of stick required for mailbox hockey is a snowplow. The actual wicket being the wing of the plow which in certain desperate climes is used at the height of winter to throw back the snow bank to make room for future deposits. It was a hilarious thing for snowplow wing-men to behead a mailbox under the guise of widening the farm road. Even more fun at thirty miles per hour and four inches of new fallen, the wing stuck out to cleverly behead the mailbox. Of course quite accidental. They always blame it on poor visibility. Besides, plowing snow all winter long is about as boring as frying bacon in hell. The crew needed some sport, needed it to keep their morale up. Mailboxes are the traditional snowplow-driver's cheer. It was a given. Wise farmers kept a spare mailbox in the granary. Knowing their time would come. It was the dues. Complainers did not get plowed out any time soon.

A person of any permanence after a while takes up the sport of mailbox hockey, of playing the game on the side of the mailbox. This is known as reprisal. In the early days the snowplow wing was operated by a set of pulleys and rope. A haw on one end of the rope drew the wing forward, a haw on the other retracted it. Once in position an inertia brake held the wing in position. Jerking hard released the brake and a haw on the retreat end of the rope swung the wing out of the way. The problem as any engineer can attest is the inertia brake. It was not intended for hazardous climates, it held the wing in position but tentatively. The wing man assisted this mechanical lack of precision by holding on to the rope. Lots of country people knew this 'cause hay forks worked the same way.

The simplest retaliation then was to bury a steel post next to the mailbox. When the wing whaps the post, the wing retreats. Pulling on the rope. At forty foot a second. The effect is an attempt to strain the wing-man through the hole originally sized only for the rope. It is like being bit by a shark. Like being swallowed by a whale, whose mouth is too small but is trying to swallow the wing-man all the same. This method doesn't work twice 'cause it is so obvious. You can count on losing your mailbox at least once a winter after this.

One of the better methods, assuming you've tried the steel post, was the milk-can/dead-cat ploy. The milk can is filled with stones ... lead shot if available ... the idea is to make it heavy ... REAL HEAVY. The milk can is buried in the snow bank at some distance from your personal mailbox, better yet, on another town road. Buried in the snow. Hidden in the snow. With a dead cat on top. Never did there live a plow crew as could resist adding insult to a dead cat. Not only is a dead cat irresistible, it lent real enthusiasm to the task of plowing snow. The truck accelerates. Hits the cat doing 45 mph. Throwing it most of a hundred yards back from the road. The crew is laughing. Slapping their legs. They ain't watching. They hit the milk can doing 45. The haw rope retreats through that little bitty hole at 60 feet per second. The wing man has gotten smart. He isn't holding the rope. It is tied to his foot. He never did find his galosh. The result of this is to thin out the wing man's thinking for a long time 'cause he doesn't know who to blame. After that some mailboxes go on to die of old age.

It didn't last. The town plow went hydraulic. But then the town plow wasn't the only hydraulic ram in the world. Every farmer has a front-end loader and soon enough discovered how hard and dense a snow bank can be made after repeated batterings, and how it still looks like an ordinary snow bank. A snowplow with the wing down hitting a knot like this in the snow bank has the town crew's attention. And then the mailbox is again safe, for a while.

What God is Like

As a kid I wondered if God was ever one. A kid, I mean. Where did God learn to make chickens? Was it the same as when I tried a crystal radio? From a kit costing ninety-nine cents in a catalog? Did God have a catalog? Did the universe come in kit form like my crystal radio? Ninety-nine cents for some really simple parts and as I remember, darn few directions, but somehow when you tickled a stone with a whisker you heard something resembling rock and roll. Perhaps it was only coincidental that the wind on the boxelder tree leaning against the woodshed roof also resembled rock and roll, and it didn't cost ninety-nine cents to try.

I never understood how that radio worked. Maybe God doesn't have to understand how to make a chicken any more than I understood how to get music and base-ball from a stone.

Kids have thoughts on God that Biblical scholars and theologians can not have. Every salesperson understands why. You can't suspect your quality carpet cleaner works more by reason of the scrub brush, which the customer already owns, than by the brightly bottled carpet cleaner and energizer.

For a long time as a kid I thought God was the wind, invisible but present; the harder the wind blew the more length of God was involved. Storms with bushels of lightning and thunder were heavy-duty doses of God. The Biblical scholar recognizes in this the classic Old Testament corollary, mistaking the smell of ozone and nitrites for the presence of God. From which we are properly chastized when we learn heathens who don't give squat for theology, appreciate God for the very same dose of industrial-strength drama. This is how come heathens prefer to worship under a tree, being it is closer to God than something with a roof. As a kid, I learned in due course that science was making the noise and not God. And if I didn't want to end up like an Easter Island savage, I best reform my ways and pray in shirt and tie like decent theological folk... who don't fall for cheap environmental tricks when it comes to God. Whose God isn't rowdy and doesn't run in the halls and never ever swims naked in the irrigation pit.

As a kid, whenever I tried to picture God, he always ended up resembling something of my Grandpa Fletcher, not all furry and agitated like Michaelangelo's God, but wearing bib overalls and sitting on a stump. Smoking a cigar.

God wore bib overalls for the same reason my Grandpa Fletcher wore bib overalls, being no end to the junk a person can pull out the pockets. Genesis happened the morning God emptied his pockets, and God didn't have to know how to make a chicken as long as the pocket did, which sorta explained things to me. Was God wearing the overalls but it was the pocket that knew what it was doing. Charles Darwin had much the same idea only he was more long-winded about it. Science and evolution happen in the pocket and God is just the poet who is wearing the grand unified set of overalls. Being a kid, I was at peace with this answer.

I have a lot of respect for kid thoughts on God. The average clergy does not give theological weight to whether cows and dogs go to heaven. The question is beneath them and they dismiss the attempt. They cannot see that heaven might be the same boring place as my maiden aunt's parlor, both of 'em overwhelmed with ovals of dead ancestors. Heaven, too, having lace doilies over every uncomfortable piece of furniture, none of it worth sitting on, and where doing anything is misbehaving.

As a kid I thought heaven ought be like the low pasture on the back side of the farm where a cold water creek runs, and it is OK after chores to fish. A heaven it was where brass hooks and fillet knives are allowed and campfires and cheap cigars. Theologians will be quick to point out that a heaven defined by trout water means mayflies and if the sun ever sets those flies will die, which is a word they don't want in their brochure.

Kids should wonder about God, and if they are wise, not tell their parents what they are thinking, parents being so darn linear. A kid can talk to God and not feel peculiar about it, this what puptents and treehouses are for. Heathens talk to trees and rocks instead of God direct 'cause they think it is more polite. Why bother God with a problem when talking to a stone is solution enough? God to a kid is not a distant agency. God don't have to be understood, just interesting and pretty to look at, which is confusing to theologians. A kid knows God cracks jokes, really gross jokes sometimes, and talks like a duck. Kids know this because they have wondered, wondered where theologians cannot.

The Haystack

The marsh was hay, at least mostly. If something less than premium hay, it was however ample. So ample was marsh hay as to think it a kind of philanthropy. Or perhaps manna from heaven. But only if you really needed the marsh hay. Manna from heaven often works like that.

Hay on the highlands could on the whim of summer drought turn disastrous and it was for this eventuality the cautious farmer maintained a couple forties as a reserve, for marsh hay. As hay, it was good enough, good enough for young stock any year, and it didn't require the premium shelter of a barn roof as did highland alfalfa. We could pile it up in great pouting monuments, Aztec-like pyramids, Scottish castles, Chinese walls, Roman coliseums… of hay, marsh hay.

On the farm where I was a bairn, beyond the barn was an open area neatly fenced where every year we piled excess marsh hay. It was a particular joy, marsh haying, because it was conducted entirely outdoors with no suffocating haymow to intervene and fill, where the light was bad and the air worse. The haystack, as a consequence, became a competition between neighbors as to who could build the tallest, the longest, the most symmetrical mountain of marsh hay. Some seeking further grandeur built their haystack over a framework of poles and boards rendering the inside hollow, the stack in turn several times larger than were it hay to the core. This may have been cheating as far as the competitive haystack was concerned but it proved benevolent in the winter when the plug was removed to reveal a remarkable internal shelter for young stock and heifers. This did not go unnoticed in our enthusiasms, so unbeknownst to our father, we built secret apartments in the haystack using boards and lath to support the ceiling. The opening known only to us was sealed over with a layer of hay bales. Secret chambers these were, of the sort the pharaoh's engineer would recognize. One chamber was equipped with a stovepipe, not for smoke but to call down light into the hidden nave. On a cold winter day after finding which bale exactly provided the access, we'd crawl down a tunnel into a burrow insulated to the highest R-factor ever encountered by human subjects this side of a mummy. A place that with the comforts of a flashlight and a burlap sack became divinely comfortable. A piece of scrap wood adorned with a facsimile of a hay bale was used to plug the tunnel so we could disappear for hours at a time. Utterly vanish. Safe from family, safe from chores, and safe from those who thought what we might be looking at was beyond our maturity to comprehend. How could a picture of Rita Hayworth or Kim Novak wearing what was darn appealing be beyond our sensibilities when it was obvious we were already acutely knowledgeable of something. If not necessarily knowing what that something was. As I remember it, the sense was rather akin to worship; though I knew even then it was an occult worship as Christians weren't supposed to find icons such as these the least bit transcendental. It was not explained to me why this was so. Neither did I ask. Some things, some transcendental things are better left unexplained. Because theology would probably botch up the business when it comes to Rita Hayworth.

Sunday afternoons were the best time, because nobody came wondering why this or that chore still wasn't done. A pocketful of cookies, a dog for company, a cap with ear flappers; thus provisioned we set out after dinner for the inner chamber. The dog whimpering with curiosity and perhaps a little fear, as we plugged the passage behind. It was necessary to worm down the narrow passage. A quality hay cave had at least a fifty-foot crawl to get to the central burrow, with several changes of elevation included and a couple wrong turns, one of which led to a trap hole over the cattle chamber. This trap was laid for the older brother who, if discovering our secret hatch, would choose the wrong turn and, because of the dark, fall among the heifers on the pile of manure. We considered this fair play at the time. Protecting the burrow from a brother who'd sure as hell try to get our incomprehensibly valuable black and white copy of Rita dressed up in high quality slink. Premium grade editions of this photograph were known to retail in the school- yard for two jackknives, a box of long rifle cartridges, and the Audubon field guide to birds. The only thing of higher value was a *Playboy* magazine itself valued at three packs of cigarettes, a bone-handled Bowie knife autographed by Davy Crockett, and the hubcap to a 1909 Stanley Steamer.

It is remarkable the degree of contemplation as can be practiced by a kid in the dark. Even better is that contemplation in the winter in a place of his own mak- ing with a dog. Sometimes I'd turn off the flashlight and just listen. Listen to the haystack. Listen to the sounds below of the cattle moving and breathing. If the wind was up, it too was noted in a stiff crustal movement of the haystack. The dog breathing rapidly at first from the excitement of crawling into a dark hole, subsided to a calm respiration as I stroked her head. Then I listened to myself. How out-loud was my heart. Buried in the hay I could hear my own blood circulate, pulsing through my veins in ungainly jerks of fatty globules from Sunday dinner, pinched to a whine by the ever-smaller vessels and capillaries. I do not think I knew what a capillary was but I had heard one.

Eventually I fell asleep, what with Mama's dinner, the warmth, and the increasing level of CO_2. To wake later in the dark womb of marsh hay, having no idea where I was or what way was up or down or how to get out. I remember wondering if I had had this same thought before, in the dark of my mother, or in the dark of God. If I wondered then, too, how to get out. I wondered if tree roots and flower buds and mushrooms felt something like what I felt in the darkness. Some dark soul shared between us, each wondering how and where to find the light. It scared me sometimes, that I might not find my way, that disoriented, that far from light. My family would not discover me until spring and I'd be mummified same as cats found buried. Dead because they couldn't hear my cries through the hay bales, lost in my own labyrinth.

The sense passed, and I knew again where I was, the dog licking my face and ready to go. We worked our way to the surface, threw open the hatch, the dog somehow wormed past in its excitement, leaped out the hole and slid to the bottom of the stack, waiting there with its tail at separate frenzy. It seemed to me that while in the haystack, days had passed, when it was but twenty minutes. Time, I believe, and science will some day concur, goes faster in the dark.

By early summer the haystack was fed out and the area raked and combed for another season. I had my pile of boards ready, 2 x 4s this time. That I would install secretly to fashion an even more interesting chamber. Something I think with a window.

The Submarine

Every kid has an Uncle Hal. I don't know with any certainty what Uncle Hal did for a living; whatever it was, it was some place in Minnesota. My mama didn't like Uncle Hal 'cause he ate like a bejesus horse. My mama didn't think nice things came from Minnesota 'cause she heard that Minnesotans went naked in the winter. For my mama going naked was bad, but going naked in the winter was not only unchristian it was jesus-crimeny strange. Uncle Hal's real name was Halifax but nobody called him that. He was just Uncle Hal from Minnesota, somewhere.

Every Christmas is not what Uncle Hal did, he was some rarer than that, an occasional kind of uncle, showing up maybe when the roads were open to where ever he was from. Uncle Hal was partial to Cadillacs, none of our other relation drove swarmy cars, that's what mama called a Cadillac. I still don't rightly know what swarmy means, sounds like something bees do. Uncle Hal's Cadillac was different... it was not just a car, it was a pickup truck. From the driver's door back to the tail fins, what had once been a four door long chassis black Cadillac was stake and rail pickup truck. That Uncle Hal did this sort of thing to a Cadillac put mama in the apprehensive mode, if a man performed this act of desecration to a

5,000-dollar Cadillac, he just might do anything. Mama was apprehensive every time Uncle Hal from somewhere in Minnesota showed up at Christmas.

He was a wide man, Uncle Hal was, his head seemed twice the size of the normal model. He wasn't fat, just big. Uncle Hal often sat on two chairs, out of favor to the chair. He wore basketball shoes all the time, high-top white-dot Keds; in those days real grown-ups never wore Keds. And he should have gotten his tooth fixed, the one missing in the middle of the top row. When he talked you couldn't help but look at that empty spot in his mouth going up and down. I don't remember anything he said exactly but I do remember his mouth saying it. Uncle Hal's hair was black and speckled, like chicken eggs are speckled, it looked mown off. Not with scissors or a clipper, I mean it looked mown off with a hay mower, none of it was the same level. My mama said he had probably done it himself with sheep shears.

Sometimes on Christmas Uncle Hal showed up. It was that which bothered my mama, the suddenness of Uncle Hal, how one minute he wasn't there and the next he was, and it all of a sudden sort as a three-ton Cadillac made into a pickup truck can induce with Uncle Hal pulling on the air horn. Yup... his Cadillac had an air horn from a Mack truck. My mama's flower garden was on the east side of the front porch; glads, mums, daisies, foxglove, dahlias, iris, maybe a wild orchid or two she had dug up from the woods. Every fall she bedded her flower plot under a layer of oat straw so stuff that wasn't supposed to bloom in Wisconsin at summer did and pretty regular. You can guess where Uncle Hal parked his Cadillac. That air cannon didn't help none and neither did the steer horns on the front grill, nor that Uncle Hal took up two chairs at the supper table and crossed himself like a crocodile does before every meal. Normally one chicken sufficed to feed mama's table, there being six of us, potatoes, string beans and boiled cabbage filled any other want. The presence of Uncle Hal meant two chickens, a peck of potatoes, it meant two pies and two of everything else. When my mama canned fruit and vegetables during the summer she held in her mind a kind of exit ratio, how many jars of tomatoes per week, how many carrots, how many bushels of potatoes, how many chickens, canned pears, canned corn, canned peaches. My mama had a kind of mileage per quart jar chart etched to her brain. A formula on which stood not only the survival of her family but absolutely the survival of the household budget and the farm's resulting liquidity when it came to acquiring next spring's seed corn and fertilizer. Uncle Hal's abrupt appearance impacted mama's cellar equation. She had no recourse but to install an Uncle Hal factor in her preparations, disallowing she already had an extra shelf in the root cellar for when Uncle Ray and his sons visited. She always said they ate like they were starving. My mama should have suffered Aunt Marion's cooking enough to know why Uncle Ray and the boys ate like "varmints." There was another shelf for stove wood, when our dad hired a couple neighbors to help in the woods, skidding saw logs, putting up wood who besides 50 cents an hour got a fine supper with several coats of reapplied paint. There was a shelf for a blizzard or three; we didn't feel we were free from marooning until the end of March, explaining why in April and May we would have peach cobbler and cherry pie almost every night, mama making room for next year's jars.

Uncle Hal's custom was to bring to the farmhouse one present, in the course of our childhood he showed up perhaps only five or six times, on each occasion bringing with him a present in the cargo hold of his converted Cadillac. One year it was a billiard table he bought from a tavern someplace. We set it up in the old ice house as wasn't used to store ice any more. Between games of basketball we shot pool, 12 below zero billiards, mama thought we liable to get from that table the habit of tavern games with implications on our soul. One year he brought my father a complete steel bar bull pen. He probably remembered the lath and wattle cage we kept the bull in, in between service calls. The next summer we poured a new cement floor in the far corner of the barn, anchoring there the full metal jacket for the farm's Holstein Casanova. Another year it was recliner for our dad that performed all forty-eleven positions of leisure. Our father did after that take his noon nap in the reclined position so his mouth didn't come open like it did before and he no longer made whale noises with his nose. We were all grateful for that recliner.

The Christmas present I remember had occurred some years earlier. I was eight, maybe nine years, my older brother 12 going on 30 and the little brother seven years. That year Uncle Hal brought us a submarine, at least sort of a submarine. It was a trunk about two feet wide and four feet long, made of white pine with brass hinges, on each end a manila rope handle. The cover of the trunk fit precisely over the bottom half, inside were books, maps and comics, the books were those subborn hard-to-burn classics; *Ivanhoe, the Virginian, Two Years Before the Mast, Huck Finn, Connecticut Yankee, Big Red, Red Badge of Courage*, Davy Crockett's diary, *Jim Bridger, Merriwether Lewis, Sitting Bull*, General Grant's Memoirs. It was years before we eventually read all those books, I have yet to read the *Punic Wars*. The maps were of the heavens, sea charts, U.S. Geological Survey maps, maritime maps for the Duluth harbor, a French map of upper Canada dated 1705, a map of China, and the Oregon Trail. Along the back side of the cover were vent holes that seemed strange on a book trunk until you realized a bottom board of the trunk slid to one side to act as a prop, on that same end of the trunk was a padded headrest over which a sliding panel revealed a tiny glass window neatly lighting the book being read if your head was in the correct position. The trunk had one further curiosity, a second sliding panel revealed a round hole two inches in diameter, inside the trunk was a cardboard tube some 14 inches long. The tube slid through the round hole and if your head was correctly positioned on the headrest, this tube became a periscope whose effective range of view was limited by how far you could crane your neck. Being farm kids we fit inside that trunk with room to spare. I have occasionally wondered whether the reason we never did grow to be normal-size men was because of that trunk or because farm chores just squashed the excess out of us.

I have wondered what kind of people we might have become without that Christmas trunk from Uncle Halifax. I first read *Ivanhoe* when I was 13 or 14, Robin Hood I crossed paths with at 10. No, it was 11 because that was the year I fell in love with Kathy Feit. The Oregon Trail was sometime later because I lived in Sherwood Forest for what must have been two years, in the farm's heifering woods I had my bowers, I made arrows of birch whips, my long bows I made of ash. Because of that submarine I went on the Silk Road with Polo, spoke Ojib with Marquette, went to die at the Alamo with Crockett and Bowie. I wonder sometimes what might have become of us without the intercession of the book submarine. I knew places a farmboy rarely goes, we took turns going under sea in our submarine, in the winter it was in the attic room beneath the window, if you put a wool blanket over the backrest before climbing in and folding down the cover, the interior became toasty warm. It gave mama the creeps, resembling to her a coffin more than a submarine.

The periscope looked better than it was useful since you could only see so much with it. Besides, my older brother wrecked the cardboard tube when he poured water down it attempting to displace me. I admit it was his turn.

One Christmas Uncle Hal's present to us was a junk Model A, weren't much body left but the engine was all there. This we assembled and disassembled somewhere going on a hundred times. If we learned from a pup tent to be unafraid of the dark, we learned from that engine to be unafraid of things mechanical.

When we had kids ourselves we took turns sharing the submarine but found one was simply insufficient to the need so we built two others of white pine and red oak; they still give mamas the creeps. My brother put a surplus tank periscope in the trunk he built, and he put in different books than I did. My kids had Ursula La Guine and Huck. His kids had the Hobbit, Mr. Roberts and C.P. Snow. I never could stand Mister Roberts and his cardigan sweaters. My brother still wears cardigan sweaters.

It all started with Uncle Halifax who sometimes came at Christmas, we'd never know whether or not. As said, five maybe six times he came. I suppose he is dead now, I don't really know if or when, during college and the war things got jumbled including Uncle Hal. Mama said he was from Minnesota, maybe a cattle dealer, as would explain the Cadillac. Coulda been a carpenter, as would explain the book box we called submarine.

A Treehouse
Called Spit

Every kid wishes at some point, and maybe not kids only, to have one thing, no matter how small, that is the best. Marketeers know this motivation and have designed all sorts of consumer labels and trash to fulfill this elementary desire. So everyone can have one thing of the very best, be it jeans, cars, timber framing, Picasso, Nike, Rembrandt, Pavarotti, Porsche, French cinema, mahogany, high fiber, Harris tweed... The list is virtually inexhaustible, which is the thing about Madison Avenue.

As a kid I had no illusion about what exactly was the best thing. The world had only recently emerged from a cruel theater as ever performed on a captive audience, and surprisingly the good guys won. The reason the good guys won was, at least in my child's estimation, due to one particular machine that during one hyperventilating and critical moment when the war might have tipped into the abyss but for this one excaliber and some guys who rode it in the middle of the sky. The moment was the Battle of Britain and the machine as single-handedly tipped the course of human events, at least for one farmkid, was the Supermarine Spitfire.

As a kid I knew this to be so, and very much so at that. Never mind a later reading suggested the Hawker Hurricane did the bulk of the business and was more capable in unskilled hands, which due to a severe shortage of pilots, unskilled hands were in some abundance. But the Hurricane never quite made the artistic grade as far as I was concerned. For me, the Spitfire was the prettiest lethal object ever designed by mankind, save the kilt and the lever action octagonal barrel Henry rifle. Castles with drawbridges were pretty neat too but not something a kid can do. And I co' no' wear a kilt til I be mon enough to knock doon any as called it a skirt, so said my grandda. A Spitfire was however within my capabilities, though I didn't ask anyone else of their opinion of my capabilities.

The basic airframe of my Spitfire began with the box-elder tree north of the ice house whose operational ceiling was 23,000 feet, same as Spit. I remember how I liked saying that word, Spit. How my mother couldn't get me to stop because it was an historical artifact and proper people, even kings and queens and Winston Churchill, said "Spit" in public. A rudimentary treehouse I had built the year before, preceeded by several others, each of them at a lower altitude than my latest creation. This last was on the final frontier of treehouses, occupying as it did the highest possible construction crotch of that tree that science knows as the aphelion. Higher even than the one I had built in the pine at the edge of Whittaker's woods, but that was for crows when I was into crows which I still was but not to the degree that I wanted to spend the summer being one, which I did before.

The raw ingredients for a Spitfire treehouse were the same as for every other treehouse except with the added emphasis of lethal appearance. Something with wings, a rudder, propeller, control stick, twin Browning machine guns, pilot's seat, compass, radio, ailerons, rudder pedals and a 12-cylinder Royce. The farm junkpile had lots of this stuff already and Myron Woods, who repaired radios and televisions for a hobby, had a junkpile with all the necessary electrics. Which is what the Brits would say, "electrics," same as they'd say "Spit" and "Winnie" and "tay." I started drinking tay that summer and found a leather winter cap that looked like enough like a flying helmet, and I found cracked welders' goggles still serviceable to an aviator and a sheepskin high altitude coat in my grandfather's closet, never mind it was still mid-July on the rest of the farm. At 23,000 feet it is 20 degrees below and mittens are a good idea. I had them too.

Of doors and boards and rain gutters I built my Spitfire, the propeller fashioned from two broken oars mounted on the shaft of a Fairbanks and Morse water pump that was a heck of a business getting into the tree. The wings stuck out beyond the treehouse and, just like on the Spit, were kinda fragile so you oughtn't walk on them. From a cupboard door I made the rudder. The control stick came from the emergency brake of a junk truck and the bare metal pilot's seat from the same. Gauges I had lots of; gauges are what really turn the average boxelder tree into a real Spitfire airplane. Find enough gauges and just about any kind of tree can start to taxi. Gauges from cars, trucks, tractors, all of them neatly inletted to a piece of birch plywood with a scroll saw. Ammeter, speedometer, voltage, oil pressure, water temperature, revs; they were all there. For the gun sight I stole a cut glass perfume bottle from my big sister's vanity and mounted it in a lath frame so when you looked through it, the split image intersected exactly 150 yards beyond, as was the optimum convergence point for the twin Brownings. For machine guns I used water pipe, the barrels sticking out the leading edge of the wings.

In the evening after barn chores and summer hay, I'd don my flying helmet and flight jacket, scale the rope ladder to my Spit, kick the engine over, then radio the tower for clearance. Just like the real Spit I couldn't see over the nose until the speed came up to 40 knots and the tail lifted. Then it was full throttle for take-off and I'd roll into a power climb to reach operational altitude, ever watchful for Messies and Fokkers same as my sister was looking for her cut glass perfume bottle.

With the sun going down I prowled the sky for bogies, the engine puttering along on lean cruise. Sometimes we'd dog fight in the twilight, the dome of the sky was salmon pink, the contrails left behind a lacey pattern of our death struggle. I caught an ME109 on a deflection shot piercing his oil cooler but let him off knowing he probably wouldn't make it across the Channel, which struck me as the Christian thing to do. There were strange moments of high chivalry like this that don't make sense in wartime but that's how us pilots maintained some degree of normalcy. It meant as consequence I couldn't claim another kill, just a probable; at this point another death didn't matter any more. I'd been an ace long ago, so many since I couldn't remember them all and it seemed to me I was now a perfect kind of death, so perfect it didn't even remember. Sometimes you're so close as to see them in the smoke-filled cockpit, struggling to get out knowing their feet were shattered by the bullets, they can't climb out on the bloody stumps, you finish 'em if you can. Some days you take them out like so many sparrows in the feed room, other times let them go. No good reason why; maybe it was their attitude, a sense of insult from the stupid way they opened up on you way too early and when a tight turn brought you around on their tail. Blast 'em to bits. Knowing he was out there, watching, Sturmfuhrer Otto in his yellow nosed 109E with his twin turbos and a variable pitch, who always flew at theoretical limit, 30,000 feet. He didn't ever join the fight, just watched. Gote in Himmel, they called him; all he did was keep count.

My fuel low, I disengage and turn for Hawking, descending quickly to 3,000 feet, it is already dark on the ground. Air speed 60 knots I slide the canopy back, the smell of the earth rises up to meet me, corn, hay fields, cow pasture. I was mortal again and quite suddenly frightened, the transformation always the same. The smell of earth brought me home and the blood and chivalry disappeared. Now all I wanted was to survive, despite knowing it was unlikely. Still, a week more would be nice, one more landing on earth, one more chance to smell cows.

The ground crew had lit the petrol barrels for my approach. In the dark I reached down with my wheels, groping for the field until the carriage touched, then rolled to a stop beside the bunker and switched off.

Mama was calling me to bed.

The Tree in the Sky

A time ago when I too was once a kid, the best place ever... was a treehouse. How I happened to have a treehouse is because my dad was cheap. A more diplomatic way of describing his motive probably exists, but would require too much research to identify. Dad maintained a pile of scrap lumber, stuff that either fell down on its own or neighbors dropped on the humongous pile behind our machine shed, glad to be rid of it. At an early age I graduated from the erector-set sort of kid to a used-boards sort of kid.

On rainy days when my dad couldn't think of anything useful or penitential, he set me to work on the garage floor straightening bent nails. There is no limit to the thinking a kid can accomplish while straightening nails. I do not know where all the nails came from in the first place but we had an ample supply. Milk cans full of bent nails. If left over-long the nails rusted together so there was nothing to do but throw the whole can away and set up another. My dad learned the benefit of pouring kerosene over his bent nail supply every now and again.

This was how it happened I had available to me the two principals of treehouse construction; I had boards and I had nails. The nails were a variable resource; I had 6-penny, shingle, 20-penny spikes, horseshoe nails and for some reason not much in between. I knew even at this inconsequential age all things are possible with an abundance of old boards and the equal of bent nails.

At distance from the farmhouse sprawled a grove of boxelder trees, as celtic and mystic a tree as ever roamed the earth. Trees too contorted ever to be called handsome, that contained not one straight sawlog, and even less use for firewood. The most absolutely good-for-nothing tree on the planet this side of the cactus. It was however for the sake of treehouses the boxelder was granted by God to honor the earth.

Like the great Darwinian process itself I evolved through various and multiple personalities of treehouses. The first was no more than a board nailed tentatively to the tree trunk, and this no farther than two feet above the ground. I remember it collapsed and I learned to be more abundant with nails.

By stages then, I worked my way up that tree; treehouse clambered over treehouse, each the product of the benevolent lumber supply. One after another I built them, prelude after prelude, until I reached the apogee of treehousedom 28 feet 9 1/2 inches off the planet where in the convergence of high branches perched my penultimate creation, leaning in turn on each of my former constructions. I had pretty much enclosed the entire tree with this, the fullest possible expression of treehouse extravagence. A treehouse to end all treehouses. The Taj Mahal of treehouses, mayhaps this the wrong illusion. The Monticello of treehouses, to whose construction and theory I was at this juncture well-apprenticed which ain't bad for a kid.

Was in the summer of 1959, the year before I was to attend Mister Houlihan's eighth-grade class which was also a pinnacle event, that I built my triumphal treehouse. Its list of appointments included a porch, a kitchen, an indoor elevator, bomb-bay, navigator's bubble and a living room complete with a 4 x 5 picture window with leaded-panes. I had somehow raised into the tree an old woodstove, my kitchen boasted a white gas range, an antique icebox, coffee pot, cupboards, sink, drain and running water. The bedroom was two stories lower, closer to the ground because at night with the wind up, sleeping high in the tree was not comforting.

The accomodations of my treehouse allowed me to live independent of the observations and instruction of my parents. The proof was my living room wall where I accumulated the covers of Life magazine that featured Marilyn Monroe, whose shape and attitude appealed to my nerve ends, for what final purpose I had the barest sense.

As a kid I had manifold reasons to retreat to the tree-house... my own comfort chief among them. The very act of scaling the cleats nailed into the boxelder, following the winding arc of those footholds, was an exhilaration. Climbing them in the dark was no trick at all. There to ponder another of the miseries of kiddom, or to gaze contentedly at the face and shape of Marilyn Monroe.

Being the middle son of three farmboys, I enjoyed the position of invisibility except for, as every middle child will recognize, those incidents where blame is apportioned. It seemed somehow my older brother could do no wrong. He never, ever screwed up. While my younger brother who was way too smart for his age could not screw up even if he did. I, of course, did so on a routine basis. Was I, while experimenting with a Ferrari fourwheel drift on the tractor, inadvertently and unbeknownst, caught the corner post of a twenty rod fence with the manure spreader. And at speed, uprooted the same four-strand length, dragging it behind me as I came into the farmyard. Its demise still unknown to me. This moment, the very moment, my entire family including some cousins were at session on the front porch. For years after I endured the epithet "Fangio." My father not so very amused as everyone else.

When something broke or burnt down, somehow I was by mere coincidence at the epicenter of the disaster. When my younger brother lost an end of a finger to a farm accident, I raised the ante by breaking my skull in a million pieces that had to be picked up from the floor and glued together. If window panes were missing, somehow it was my BB gun as did it. And I, the last one at the gate where the cows got out. Entirely coincidental bum raps they were, which the legal system of families, to thwart unnecessary litigation, simply allocate on the middle kid.

My childhood was not the least bit traumatic, instead rather blissful, however much I enjoyed testing the Formula One qualities of the Allis Chalmers. There was the time I discovered what homemade black powder did to an old stump in the cow pasture. How the echo of that detonation lasted and lasted and lasted, and somehow my dad knew it was me straight off.

Being both a farmkid and a middle kid, I came to hate Christmas in an adult-like fashion at an early age. Christmas struck me as the most replete example of the human desire for good, yet that good seemed ever beyond our ability to secure. Christmas was somewhere between plucked heart-strings, crass extravagence, and naked greed. Such a smash-up Christmas was, between giving and receiving, yet at the same time desiring to find equilibrium with our want. I doubted God more because of Christmas than any other sin the deity committed on the human race. How the story calls up every caring person to be the Christ, the peacemaker and the brother to all living things and to dwell softly on the earth, and not be afraid to sing out loud or write poems or swim in the irrigation pit. Yet denies each that opportunity because we have no responsibility to the manger because some kid already is it. God, I thought, had screwed up Christmas... he probably a middle kid, too.

As usual the week before Christmas I mucked up again. I remember roaring down the alleyway in the barn with the silage cart, doing a spin-steer at the turn, blazing down the ramp to the opposite side of the barn and in the process knocking off the main wheels inclusive of the axle, the support plate and the bottom boards of the silage cart. Not good. Certainly not the week before Christmas and Dad having to do his shopping yet, and string lights at the church and get the last of the corn picked and the firewood up; besides milking cows and a few other chores.

Dad looked at me the look that dads can exert, as took three million years off my hide. His look shut me up, despite that I had an excuse at the ready. Like the nails holding the bottom of the silage cart had rusted through cause of silo acids and how this was bound to happen. 'Course it did happen to me. Meaning new boards on the silage cart, and taking the time to do the job which were at a premium during the Christmas pell-mell.

The week came and went and I felt miserable and quiet, which I normally wasn't. On Christmas Eve I excused myself from going to the church service 'cause of a stomach ache; frankly my stomach never ached. My dad didn't go so he could finish something in the barn, he said, "with the barn cleaner." I retired to the treehouse, built a fire in the stove, put a candle in the window and tried to think Christmas thoughts. The darkness, a routine of country night, is somehow deeper on Christmas Eve. Across the fields the neighbor's barn stood out like a cruise ship, the stars glimmered or whatever stars do, Venus dangled above the horizon fat and unblinking as a goose egg. I sat at the treehouse window, put my ear flappers down and gazed at the scene, thinking one day I would like to farm just to claim this scene, to hold these fields and their relationship with the stars. So absorbed I was I did not notice my father's entry into the treehouse. He climbed the cleats in the dark like he been this way before. Like maybe he had been watching over this place where I stored my heart.

He said something the equal of "ease-up" in the present vernacular and I slid over to make room for him on the bench by the window.

"Nice," he said.

"You know how to climb the tree in the dark?"

"Yup."

"Been here before?"

"Yup."

"How come?"

"Nice place," he said.

"What does looking across the fields make you feel?" he asked. I recognized this as a wide sort of question, to which there are two answers; one for other times, one for Christmas.

"Like God feels," I replied.

"Yah," he said.

"Dad, I'm sorry about the silage cart."

"Was gonna go anyway."

"But..."

"'S OK... 's OK," he said again, laying his hand on my leg. "It needed new bottom boards anyway. I just finished them and want you to know that is my Christmas to you."

"But I was gonna do it for you at vacation."

"I know," he said, "but I wanted to do for you first."

I remember getting that feeling I particularly resent, so bubbly and frothy warm it makes me feel almost like a girl. When all the nerves on one side of your face tingle and go bumpy, your insides real mushy, and if nobody was watching you'd set to having a good bawl.

"I brought something for your treehouse," and Dad

went to the porch and heaved on the rope. On it was the end of balsam we had set up in the house the previous day, and as part of the farmhouse tradition, was three foot over long.

"I thought it'd look nice up here." Dad had nailed a couple scraps of lumber to the trunk so it sorta stood upright. From his pocket he produced a pack of birthday candles and modeling clay.   We smushed a dab of clay to the branches and stuck a candle to it, and when the candles were all in place he took out a couple kitchen matches, and he and I lit each and every candle.

He motioned to me and we climbed down from the tree. He guiding my feet to the cleats even though I knew them, but it felt good to have his hands touch my feet as we descended the dark.

From below we looked up at the tree in the sky. Neither of us said anything. The tree was pretty enough in that oversize window, but what we both saw were the pictures of Marilyn Monroe on the back wall, how the flickering shadows of candlelight seemed to make them hover and flit. Her shape, her face, her countenance appeared and disappeared in a curious sort of way. Angelic even.

Dad touched my shoulder, "When you're done at the treehouse, maybe you would help me wrap your mama's Christmas present."

That year Mama got a slippery lingerie thing we could hardly get to lay still, was kinda like trying to hold water, for so did it want to flow in your hands. The costume almost exactly resembled the one Marilyn wore on the cover of Life magazine. I folded the corners of the tissue paper while Dad taped them down. We used electrical tape 'cause we couldn't find the regular stuff. I recall feeling the same thing I felt at the treehouse, when looking over the dark fields and the neighbor's backside, and believing you know something wise.

When is a Kid Old Enough?

When is a farmkid old enough to drive a tractor? Farmers have learned not to ask this question in mixed company because one of the harder fought battles of the sexes is over the tractor and when a kid is old enough. At what age a child is physically and mentally ready to drive a tractor has three correct answers. One is the female answer, another is the politically correct safety institute answer, of a different opinion is the overall lobby. The author will not detail for the reader how he knows any of this. As we might guess the answer is a compromise.

Farm safety experts have their answer to the question, it is closer to the female. It comes with the graphs, the behavioral profiles, the motor-skill tests and an off-farm sense of safety. Safety experts do not have the same estimate of a wagon tractor as does the farmer, the expert sees it as a mechanical object larger than a lawn mower, hence correspondingly more dangerous. The farmer on the other hand begins his safety sense at the city limits which gives him the creeps and diminishes inversely with mean distance.

I was 5 when I drove a tractor sitting on my father's lap,

an 8N Ford on the marsh road which was real long, real straight and real lonely. Pa worked the pedals, I held the wheel, we were in third gear at 700 rpm, maybe 4 mph.

Modern safety folks would have arrested my father for child abuse... a child on a tractor without a seat belt, open tractor, no roll bar... the man should be ashamed of his cruelty. Neither my dad nor I told mother about driving the tractor because even in those ancient days we both understood the politics of tractors.

At what age a kid is ready to drive requires straight talking and it isn't appropriate for farmers to concede the rhetoric of the debate to the politically-correct, the uptown, the farm safety expert, or even Mama. To the non-ag community any age short of the 14-15 range is too young. They read the paper and note the incidence of injury and death, what the experts have to say; in sum an urban sensibility. Contact football is not perceived as the same kind of danger, nor are gymnastics, mountain bikes, roller blades, skateboards, surf boards or skiing, yet we read in the paper of injury and death.

Every person's sense of threat is a corresponding measure of their unfamiliarity. The farm population is not threatened by the gothic leviathans as are modern tractors because they are an everyday experience and part of our comfort level. Urban sensibilities and safety experts and some farm wives look at tractors as decidedly monstrous, surely intimidating, some with nurse tanks and duals are downright scary. So who is right about when a kid is old enough?

Every kid is different; so are tractors, as are the labor demands on the farm, its geological setting, the strength and acuity of the kid, the agreement between the farm partners and marriage partners, add also when local tradition says it is OK for a kid to drive.

The answer is a compromise between what Mama, the

graphs, the news clippings and Dad thinks is the right age, maybe too the kid.

It depends on what we mean by drive. Sitting on a lap steering is one thing; pulling a forage box down the highway in high gear is another. Going after cows on a Farmall Cub is driving a tractor but how much different from going after cows in an ATV? Which is safer? Which is perceived safer? The mechanical safety of the tractor enters into the discussion. A clapped-up pile of rust without brakes may look less dangerous than the big thing, but is it? Can the kid effectively reach the pedals? Has he/she been genuinely trained? Is the chore they are to perform straightforward? Will they encounter traffic or hazards such as steep terrain? Has the importance of safety been discussed with them? Do they know what every knob and lever is for and demonstrated their knowledge? Does the farm have "learner-tractors?" Is there a pattern of chores where tractor skills can develop progressively? Does an adult have time to teach these skills? Is there an empty pasture where kids can learn to steer around obstacles, learn to back up a trailer or negotiate corners with a tractor, chopper and wagon, or is the first time for real?

There is no exact right age when a farmkid is old enough to drive. Every farm situation, every child is different, so too the mix of tractors, types of agriculture involved, farm location, the season, the crops. The fears and values every farm family brings to the question are different, so too are our comfort levels. If Dad has nightmares, maybe the kid is too young.

Sure there are farmers who rush their kids into tractor driving. Just as there are neighbors and onlookers who see a kid in the cab of a tractor and note how out-of-proportion the kid is, and absolutely how he/she is way too young. Who is right? Farm parents must qualify their answers with the kid and a reasonable expectation of competency.

It is altogether right that farmers recognize their lives are on a different plane than safety experts. We have no built-in retirement plans, no paid vacations, no government job securities, there is no tenure in our classroom. Kids helping with chores and field work markedly improve profitability, this has been the unspoken by-law of agriculture since the thigh-bone plowshare. Farmkids are not the item same found in the suburbs, early on they become part of the business function and every farmer knows why.

When is a kid old enough to drive a tractor? There is no right answer. Every farmer has to chew this himself, the incidents reported in the newspaper are reason enough to think carefully because forgiving yourself for a life-taking accident isn't possible. Not when it was a kid.

The Holler that Came Looking for Us

It was late when we came home. Passing through the village the street lights, gas stations and hamburger joints cut a warm path through the dark.

The son asked, did you ever play baseball at night?

The question closed on me like a spring trap and suddenly I was dangling on the end of a memory; of baseball, farm baseball, farm night ball when the farm and all to which it belonged and needed was light years from anything. Farm night baseball required no incandescent fixtures. We were less afraid of the dark then; besides, darkness was part of the game. To the son I said, we played nightball.

Widow Soik's land was in the Soil Bank except for the forty by the irrigation pit where she, Uncle Walt and the boys raised potatoes sold on the market square. That her sons were in exact age sequence to my brothers and I served as a fundamental ingredient to our every enterprize, nightball included. For a while this precise duality between the families confounded my understanding, so close were our ages and zeals it seemed a greater force was involved in the existence of farm boys not creditable to chance alone. Between the two families we mustered

five boys to any baseball game. The number is inappro-
priate to baseball but we had two farm dogs the equal of
any minor league outfielder. One was a somewhat pure
border collie and the other a rogue white springer whose
tail had been inexpertly bobbed. Cut too long and the dog
had as a result less a bob than an eight inch black-jack.

Nightball in the township was a foregone conclusion
because the days were universally devoted to hay fields,
potato ground, calf pens, chicken coops and various
other ills now either constitutionally or mechanically
subtracted from the lives and limbs of farm kids. The
result of electric motors and hydraulic pumps rather than
liberal legislation, this mechanical service once was the
sole purpose of farmboys. The hour for baseball came
after evening chores, under a sky caught between day
and night, filled now with radiant ethers, this what we
took for illumination.

A portion of the Widow Soik's Soil Bank field was
seized for a ball diamond, trimmed with a hay mower
once a week and was a handsome park by township standards. Four cedar poles from a derelict corn crib served
as a backstop, the uprights covered with chickenwire,
also derelict, and nailed home using the staples from
our fence-buckets. On the farm everyone had their own
fence bucket. Pa's fence bucket had the new staples and a
pair of "Universal Chore" fence pliers and a hex-headed
hammer we were warned never to use. The fence hammer was like his personal armament, his Excaliber, his
claymore, and with this he defended the farm borders.
The hammer had his balance in it and we knew damn well
not to touch it. Our own fence-buckets were filled with
used staples, insulators, clip wire and a hammer whose
sore face had mushroomed from previous violences. In
truth the wide hammer served our purpose better than
Pa's carbon steel, all we had to do was flail away know-

ing the hammer would in all mathematical probability smack the staple. Which is a tough thing when you're but 96 pounds, spit included, and stretching 16 miles of barbwire in one hand and attempting to plant a first staple with the other.

Pa's recalcitrance for our using his bucket was our habit, according to him, of losing his stuff. So maybe we didn't know where his best chrome-plated pliers were. We did know which field they were lost in and some day we'd find them with the hay baler. Hadn't we discovered all sorts of stuff in hay bales lost by other generations? Rob Berry once found a rolling block Remington while baling second crop. The wood stock was gone but the rest looked like a gun even though it was pretty much glued together. We decided 'mong ourselves this was the very gun the Courtwright brothers had used to kill Sheriff Baker and we wondered if they could do ballistics on a gun that had done time in a hayfield. We wondered if they took the bullet out of the skull of Sheriff Baker. Probably didn't. Ballistics weren't necessary to know who shot the sheriff when the onlyest people shooting at him were the Courtwrights. The bullet is probably still in his box at Yellow Banks. We thought to check this out since Jimmy Soik had a microscope and all we needed was that bullet from the skull of the sheriff and that gun Rob Berry found on the marsh slope of his west forty. Kinda ruined the storyline of our plot when we found out the sheriff had been shot in the stomach.

Jimmy Soik measured off the ball diamond. Walked the outside rim of the playing field a couple of times till there was sign enough to follow with the mower. The next night after chores we raked the hay and baled it, dug postholes for the backstop, nailed on the screen and filled potato bags with sand for the three bases. Home plate was a silo hatch, being more cresote than wood a summer buried in the ground won't hurt it none especially if Pa didn't find out. The rungs on the down side served to anchor the silo hatch which is why we had to bury it. Besides, home plate is always buried. Thing weighed near a hundred pounds, 70 of that being creosote. A silo hatch is some bigger than regulation home plate, the point being all we had available was the silo hatch. Besides, when you're playing overhand without an umpire, a wide dose of home plate is vital to getting somewhere else than a fist fight over whether or not the pitch was a strike or not. With five kids and two dogs divided into two teams meant nothing left over to act as umpire. Same way the farm was, a sense of living where no umpire counts the strikes, balls and foul balls. To play fair we had to have the umpire inside us.

We played night ball. Thing about night ball is any sort of hit in the outfield was good for a double, that is if you can see it well enough to hit it in the first place. We kept an ice cream pail of barn lime behind the backstop to roll the ball in and whiten it some. When you hit the ball it gave a visual snort and left a contrail to follow against the dark. The barn-lime flavored ball also kept the dogs from running off with it.

The rules changed as the light went. Overhand is pretty much homicide when you can't see the ball. But with anything more than a quarter moon night ball could go forever. One game in '57 ended with a score of 58 to 56 and the only reason we quit was 'cause the ball went foul and landed in the ditch among the boxelders where moonlight can't touch bottom. Pa's holler from the front porch mighta had something to do with it too. I always hated it when Pa hollered that way. Not 'cause we had to go home. That weren't the reason; fact is we were ready to go home. The reason I didn't like it was 'cause nobody with a voice like Pa's ever called the Soik boys home. Widow Soik sometimes drove the car down and called from the window. Much as I loved baseball, I loved it when Pa's voice hung from the flank of the barn and brought us home after 42 innings of baseball.

I felt like one of the cows when he called. Lifted by my name toward home, raised up at the sound of his voice coming across the fields. Hear it turn sideways off the barn and flare out across the fields looking for us. Sometimes I thought some of Pa's call must've landed on the moon the way it touched everything while searching for us. Once I asked Dad if he could add the Soik boys to ours when he hollered. I wanted them to hear their names man-hollered, hear their names drift west and echo from the woods, and maybe even the moon.

Surplus Hay

We once built a sauna out of hay bales; it didn't last. Hay was the thing the farm had in surplus besides chores.

The big barn... that gambrel could... when filled with disregard to human safety... hold the first crop and half the second. Which is why my father built the new barn, of laminated spans and a lot easier to fill than the old cruck barn. This barn held the remainder of the second crop. Sometimes the second crop went wild, sometimes the rain came right, the sun stayed high and the hay went nuts. Meant hay was piled outside in a stack designed to curtail rot, its sides sloped and a trench dug around the base to keep it drained. But the hay kept coming, so we put some in the relic barn a couple miles away. It was a Civil War era barn with beams the size of black bears. Had tarpaper for a roof and that only sometimes worked. The hay stored outdoors in a stack had a better chance at surviving intact as the hay in that barn.

Surplus hay is a contagious disease; if we had it, so did everyone else. Hence the chance of selling the extra was small. The problem then was to get rid of the hay without actually wasting it. To this end our dad bought extra heifers and kept more of the bull calves in hope they would consume the surplus. Liberal amounts of hay were used to bank the potato shed even if it didn't have potatoes in it. We also banked all three walls of the milkhouse, then put a layer or two over the septic tank. When hay goes surplus you can see the result everywhere. People become extravagant, free spenders... of hay. Hay is piled alongside garages and porches. Even the doghouses have hay bales. In any regular winter hay bales flanked the west side of farmhouses; at surplus, the milkhouse is entombed by hay bales. Two layers, sometimes three. Neighbors boasted of heating the house all winter on six corncobs and a kitchen match. Those who really wanted to show off used alfalfa for insulation, some even went so far as to use second crop alfalfa, which was like using a Rolls Royce for a tow truck. Our dad, who ordinarily didn't do such a thing, put out hay for deer, but did so after dark in case the neighbors might see him; this behavior wasn't considered farmerly. We even banked up the west wall of the kirkhouse and it used only once a week. Now that was luxury.

It is not that our father told us explicitly, but we gathered from the evidence that any method we could devise to adjourn the surplus hay was OK so long as the neighbors didn't see it. We knew that. This was a secret commandment at our house, not that anybody said so in so many words but we understood, which is how it is with real commandments. They don't have to be said 'cause you're supposed to know it without it being said. Which sounds complicated but wasn't. If in doubt, don't do it next to the road. Doing semi-civilized things in pitch dark three quarters of a mile from the town road that goes pretty much of nowhere was still too public, especially if it was one of those "maybe" commandments. Word got around our neighborhood a lot faster than Silicon Valley can brag for its computers. It was an advanced form of telepathy. Instant was the communication when someone saw someone else doing something semi-weird. This of people in our township who didn't know who was the current president of the United States, yet knew what the neighbor's kids were up to, particularly if those kids hadn't taken steps to secure their antics. That's the word my dad used whenever he found out from the neighbor what we had been up to. Antics. We didn't just do stuff, we did antics. "So, what antics you been up to now?" he'd ask. It usually wasn't good news when he asked.

Actually, it wasn't our fault. Was the hay's fault, hay in surplus. All we did was poke a steel rod through the center of a round hay bale, tied a rope to each end forming a long yoke and then suspended this yoke from a rope attached to a healthy length of elm. The limb so high off the ground to get the rope around it that we shot an arrow over it trailing a fishing line. The result was a swing. So maybe not what the schoolyard would call a swing, or the PTA, but it was still a swing. Nothing antic about it at all, just a simple swing. Granted, a long arc kinda swooping swing, with a hay bale attached. We did put a good western saddle on the hay bale; still it was just a swing. The arc of the swing did go over the creek. Over a pool of water and frogs six feet deep. A swing using a hay bale with the saddle attached.

We thought we were far enough from the town road not to be seen, but the water is cold so the neighbor probably heard our squeals when we fell in. Still, it was a half mile back with a bunch of trees intervening. Dense, obliterating trees behind which you could have married the pope to a mule and nobody'd see. Except our neighbors. We suspected one neighbor had a pair of binoculars in his pickup just so he could spy on our antics. Was he who told our dad we weren't wearing clothes, which takes a steady hand on a pair of binoculars at that distance.

The wierdest thing I ever personally did with the surplus hay was build an igloo where the wind deposited a huge snow bank. I had previously attempted to build a regulation snow block igloo but noted soon after that it lacked permanence. Was then I remembered the old barn across the road was full of surplus, all I had to do was load up extra bales when feeding the young stock. This how it happened I built an igloo out of hay bales. To warm it I built a fire which was fine until I decided the fire was too small. Somehow the hay caught on fire and I didn't notice it, being the smoke hole wasn't all that good at scavanging the smoke anyway. When I left my igloo that day everything looked all right. It wasn't.

At 2 a.m. the neighbor called my dad and said a meteorite had landed in our heifer pasture and was still on fire, maybe he oughta go check. My dad tried to suggest to him that a meteorite wasn't a major liability in the middle of the winter. The neighbor somehow impressed on my dad the fire might spread, then he'd have to call the fire department and the sheriff. Our dad was smart enough to realize there was a high possibility of an alternative interpretation. That he better check it out himself despite it was 2 a.m., in the middle of the winter. 'Cause the neighbor mentioned calling the sheriff. Chalk up another antic.

So what sort of person lies awake at night looking over a heifer pasture? When I was a farmkid the neighborhood had what seemed to me a surplus of persons like that. Who knew what you were doing before you even did it. Who thought a kid going skinny down at the creek was against the commandments or at the very least the Constitution. Who ain't probably ever ridden a saddled-up hay bale across an arc of sky with more sense of freedom than an angel with its leash removed. As kids we never did build that moon rocket we planned, neither the Indianapolis race car, but we did build a swing from an elm tree. A heaven-rubbing elm tree that shaded God's own chair. Had a rope attached. And a hay bale. Surplus hay.

Kid Thoughts

The Bible omitted the Jurassic event. Metaphorically, perhaps the Deluge fits the extinction profile, if not quite so entirely hostile as a meteor the size of Chicago hitting somewhere along the coast of Guatemala 61 million years ago. I do not know why extinction events are so captivating to kids, to farmkids, to those who may yet be kids. Still, human social history is no different from biological history; we love the massacre and annihilation. We date our place in time according to some chronological demise, if for no other reason than to prepare ourselves. And understand, whether intuitively, wisely or reluctantly, that doom happens to people and good creatures.

Every kid growing up in the last three generations knows in their heart of hearts that dinosaurs were good creatures. Never mind some were flesh-eating predators, at least for them it was supper not war, if the occasional cannibal. In my youth there were not many dinosaurs to choose from; they were mostly dull gray animals, a bit ponderous, not smart, not quick, who lived in a barely plausible nature of tree ferns and volcanoes. None seemed terribly numerous. But kids loved dinosaurs, gravitated toward dinosaurs, wondered about dinosaurs, cared about dinosaurs because they were so different, so big, so alive and yet so extinct.

Our view of the ages of dinosaurs has changed considerably from the bleak gray environ once imagined. Instead of slow, simple animals crudely articulated, we now know the dinosaurs were numerous to the point of herds, continental migration and breeding hierarchy. They were brightly hued, some with scales, some with fur, some with feathers, all of it seemingly interchangeable. They ran as fast as any land creature is now capable, they leaped, jumped, frolicked, nested, cared for their children and if it hadn't been for a patch of lousy luck, the age of dinosaurs might have achieved intelligence, tools, fire, upright pianos and barbecue sauce long before that tree-dwelling rat. That, had history been fair, would now be considered a delicate table fare, tasting rather like chicken, which dinosaurs being kindred wouldn't eat. Had things been different it might have been the tree rat as went extinct due to over-hunting. Being conspicuously nude it was unlikely to flourish anyway causing one to wonder what nature had in mind with such an outrageous experiment. They too will ruminate how it is a sad commentary on the ethics of saurians that a homey little creature was allowed to die out, especially when it was so delicious. It was on their way to paved civilization that the comet intervened and dinosaurs died and whatever they might have become.

Currently the exciting research among dinosaur detritus is over the question of flight. Though birds have long been discounted as offspring of the dinosaur age, a growing body of evidence is ever more convincing as to this connection. Birds and many dinosaurs are anatomically similar, in fact similar is not quite the right word, identical may be more appropriate. Any detailed list of these similarities is disturbingly long, particularly for those who'd rather not imagine dinosaurs somehow escaping extinction. Neither is it good social policy to describe what appears to be annotated documentation that extinction is good for business, retiring species who dominated perhaps far too long, releasing in turn the prospects of those otherwise underfoot. So how similar were birds and dinosaurs? The list of shared biological priorities is long and amazing; egg-laying, the pelvic girdle, a two-chambered heart, highly sinused skulls, bipedal locomotion, reconfigured fore-limbs, migration, mass formations, nesting, binocular vision, sinus drainage, salt elimination, and now it is evident some dinosaurs had feathers. For a very long time this was in doubt; the discovery of archaeopteryx cemented the idea of a possible flight connection but the feather's specific utility was not proved. Still this "first bird" established a new direction and thinking about dinosaurs, as creatures who were for some reason using feathers. Why seems a fair question to ask. The answer to this query has fundamentally redrafted our long-established sense of dinosaurs as plodding, cold-blooded and dull. If feathers weren't for flight what other use could be made of them? The answer is obvious to a farmkid who has observed the behavior of ducks, chickens or geese subjected to cold temperatures. Pin feathers, the bane of those who still pluck their own supper, are muscle-equipped quills that at low temperatures stand upright, in turn adding loft to the overlying feathers. In modern home construction this is called the R-factor. For birds... turkey, goose, duck and chicken, blue jay and sandhill... this is the ability to adjust their R-factor. Dinosaurs with feathers probably did the same, meaning they lived where it was cold. Which in turn shatters another established mental picture of dinosaurs as only the creature of the hot humid jungle. Instead, they too were creatures of the high plain, mountains and the arctic fringe, explaining why they might have migrated.

The feathered dinosaur capable of true flight has not yet been found. A recent theory is that feathered dinosaurs used their wings as do young quail, not to fly exactly but instead propel themselves up gradients they are otherwise incapable of surmounting. Thanks to the new politic, China has opened the dinosaur record as it has never been examined before. For reasons of climate, geology and inaccessibility, China's dinosaur rich desert is the most extensive treasury of fossil record yet found. Perhaps a true flying dinosaur will be found and we will have that connective tissue between the extinction event and the present age. Ever the child, I am most disappointed that pterodactyls did not make the transition. Much as is my admiration and love for filthy dinosaurs, the opulence of the pterodactyls, those flying dragons is unequaled anywhere else in creation. Were I the God of hosts and apocalypse, that is the one creature I'd have spared and made in the course of eons the one chosen to be wise and literary. Forget *Homo sapiens, Homo erectus, Australopithecus,* mere fodder for the leather-winged luftwaffe as were pterodactyls. Imagine now a cultured form of this flying lizard. We, its progeny, would roost instead of sleep in beds. We would have explored the world in half the time, that it was round too obvious to mention. Our pterodactyl Columbus would have flown to the New World millions of years ago, and crossing the Bering Land Bridge was no big deal. Travel, tourism, locomotion in a pterodactyl world would be... well, fabulous... though I suspect engines of some sort would by now be added. Cars as we know them need never have happened, neither gridlock, greenhouse or the Arab Emirets. I suspect a body size of about the same proportions as we are now though weighing considerably less if you want to get off the ground, heart disease as a consequence unheard of.

Fire is of course required, civilization even for pterodactyls is fire and tools. We might however have been slower
to fire than was the naked ape, as a result we could still
eat raw meat with better effect and wouldn't need all
those kitchen appliances.

Losing the pterodactyl was the major single mistake of
Nature, and if science and godliness mean anything at all,
genetic therapy will address and remedy this some day.
I personally will donate my DNA, my cells, my body as
an experimental aircraft in hope of repairing this evolution inequity. I'm sure I speak for all farmkids when I
say candidly, give me back my wings.

Hubcap: The Dog from Outer Space

Was the aunt from Chicago who voiced the accusation: "Where'd that dog come from? Outer space?"

Her reference being to Ol' Hubcap, a farmdog whose ancestors had been substituted for cannonballs and fired into the rigging of the Spannish Armada, a precursor I suppose of the smart bomb. The breed had everything required of a species save one; while it lacked not the instinct for survival, omitted was any allegience to surviving in one self-same piece.

Farmdogs, as everyone knows, live vigorous lives. One look at Hubcap made this plain. The vigor of his occupation had shorn him (least he started out as a him) of major parcels of his real estate. Most dogs are four-legged and so was Hubcap. At least once upon a time. For a while he went three-legged, which ain't nothing for a dog and is almost expected of a farmdog. Then came the incident with the hammermill when he became a decimal point dog. Close as we could figure, a 2.74 legged dog. This before the mishap with the barn cleaner and the big sliding door. Hubcap was now a 2.38 dog.

Farm medicine predates the surgical adventures of

Michael DeBaky who replaced the human heart with a hydraulic pump from a tractor. Our ministry to Hubcap was no different, an elm branch and saddle-leather prosthesis belted to Hubcap's thigh alleviated the tilt that is the like result of a 2.38 dog.

This dog was born to die violently, the most jig-sawed animal you ever lay eyes on; his first leg vanished before a hay mower. Hubcap shoulda known better than tailgate a gopher who suckered that mule-headed pooch right in front of an Allis Chalmers side-mount, lickeddy-split went the leg. Snipped off cleaner than an icicle, just above the dew claw. We sutured the wound closed with harness thread and Hubcap crawled under the porch to recuperate.

Everybody knows a dog's ear is over-designed anyhow. Hubcap's ears resembled bearskin rugs more than ears, way too big for utility. A V-belt got the one and the other had an argument with a recoil starter, the remnants of each now on different wavelengths. It never ceased to amaze us what clean surgery a blunt instrument can perform.

The farm in those days was enjoying the new ministry of the alternating current motor, every previous and slave-holding chore was transformed by the application of this good humored dynamo. The farmstead soon became rigged with jack shafts, overhead roundels festooned with pulleys, coupled to flat belts that stammered and flapped. If a body didn't keep their fingers well tucked, they were liable to become part of the enterprize. Being the first generation exposed to this labor-saving, Hubcap had a hard time acclimatizing to the mechanical farm. What was left of the other ear went the way of a bevel gear, in reality a meat-grinder put to sundry other duties. Only bled a little then nicely healed over. That dog was one fast healer.

As said, when it came to medicine the farm was home-made, veterinary was reserved for the milk cows who were allied with hard cash. Hubcap wasn't and neither were farmboys. Farmgirls were different 'cause they could sometimes be traded for something useful. The rest of us got what health care the kitchen drawer provided; what a jackknife, tin snips and a drill press could fix. Add clean rags, rubbing alcohol and modern medicine had nothing on us.

Hubcap lost his right eye to the wire stretcher, a vile looking contraption capable of stringing a quarter mile of barb wire tighter than a concert violin. A good fence kinda sizzles in the wind so cows know better than even try. Don't need electric fence if barb wire is pulled up to pitch. This is some bit hazardous should the wire break and come whipping back, a quarter mile strand with trout hooks attached. The wire caught Hubcap's eye and scooped it out and we went looking for harness thread again. His tail left by monthly installments. The fancy end caught in a propeller shaft, a section was lost at the silo filler, an undignified elbow added to the stub when it was hammered over by a cast iron door, the result resembled a low-gain antenna protruding from an experimental aircraft.

The strangest thing was Hubcap's nose. He was always putting it into some essence or other; that dog had a half pint of Frenchman in him. One time he did this to the guillotine potato-seed cutter honed every morning and sharper than Solome's smile. We stitched on the red cap from a talcom powder can. As I said before, the recuperative power of this dog could fill volumes if the medical community was the least bit interested in the possibilities of unetherized harness thread.

I would relate how Hubcap died but decency prevents it. Most farmdogs go out with dignity and do the busi-

ness in private. Not Hubcap. I can only say it wasn't
the first eighteen-wheeler as killed him, neither was it
the snow-plow right behind. Nor the Airstream driven
by the retired couple from Fairfax, Virginia. Ol' Hubcap
had the survival instinct of a cannonball. It wasn't until
his ectoplasm was a thin gummy layer evenly distributed
over the next quarter mile that Hubcap quit barking. I
was tempted to sweep up what I could in a milk bucket
but that wouldna been right. Knowing Hubcap, he'd
feel obligated to get himself together. So I left him, his
molecules spreading with each passing car.

Every now and then in the middle of the night I think
I hear Hubcap pawing on the door. He still had one
regulation paw when he died. I gave thought to pickling
it but feared he'd scratch at the mason jar at 4:30 in the
morning when he liked to make his rounds.

As a farmkid, I had determined resurrection was a
pathological lie until Hubcap came along. That dog died
more times and in more ways than you could shake a stick
at, and kept coming back for more. I realize it ain't proper
to take moral instruction from a dog, and certainly not
from a from wide angle breed like Hubcap. And I want
you to know farmers have a hard time with all this resurrection, transmortal mogrification stuff anyway; besides
deciphering what has soul and what doesn't. It may be
blame clear in the village but it ain't so blame obvious in
the township. God coulda been a dinosaur fancier for
all I care and still done a satisfactory job. Made a body
wonder whether the Bible had it right when it editorial-
ized about Man fabricated in the image, you know… of
God. 'Course maybe it's just talking the raw ingredients.
About the mud puddle as the image, not mankind.

Like I was saying, sometimes I hear Hubcap in the
night, the pitter-pat-thump when he was three-legged
and the pitter-thump-thump when he was 2.38.

Why Mama
Hated Christmas

My mama hated Christmas. The reason was spoons, every Christmas since the Fall of Troy the family played spoon. Never mind no scholar can find mention of the game in the *Iliad*. They are wrong. The scholars are wrong because the way my family takes to spoon you know it's a deep-rooted phenomenon same as freckles and popcorn. Mama wouldna minded cannibalism half so much as she minded spoon.

Unlike every other card game, spoon requires no organized brain function to participate, straightforward enough for an imbecile which is exactly what my family was looking for.

The sport of spoon is a combination of poker, karate, Indian wrestling, trench warfare, jousting, metalurgy and armed robbery. It is played with a deck of cards, two decks if more than six contestants, and spoons enough to equal one less than the total number of players. Each contestant is dealt four cards held in such a manner so others can not see the hand; some members of my family have to be told this... repeatedly. The object is to acquire four of a kind, to wit a card is withdrawn from the deck and passed clockwise, each succeeding player either holds it or discards to his neighbor. The dealer fuels the frenzy by passing cards one at a time from the deck as fast as possible.

The game quickly acquires a noise level equivalent to gunnery practice as players slap down cards on the table with malevolent force. The challenge thus to watch both the hand and attend to the status of the pile of spoons in the middle of the table. The game continues until someone gains four of a kind at which point they reach for a spoon, the others seeing the intent make a grab.

Spoon is not like other card games. It has no build-up, instead throwing sparks from the onset at a pace found in no other indoor contest. There are feints to spook the opposition into a grab which eliminates them by rule. Some players don't even look at their cards, instead gaze intently at the spoons. Central to all this is the elimination of one player every round, continuing until a champion remains.

Originally the game was invented to entertain brain-damaged veterans following the Battle of Hastings, my family devoted to it ever since, and this why Mama hated Christmas. Every Christmas since Peking Man we set up the card table soon as the feast beast had been disassembled, the combatants retired to the parlor with the same much-worn and reverend deck passed down from King David, the set of spoons inherited from Mary of Scots kept in their very own felt-lined box, the same care other folks give a set of dueling pistols. Occasionally the regulation combat spoons were misplaced and we used Mama's Oneida Community table service instead; explaining why my mama hated Christmas.

Christmas at the farmhouse was like open house at the neighborhood zoo. My grandparents were there, so was the hired man and his newly paroled brother, also Harvey Peets who helped at tater season who didn't have any family, least none who wanted him around at Christmas. All my uncles were there; Kingsley and Curtis and Jim and Dean and Ray who was a Democrat.

Spoon is not a sport for womankind which didn't include my sister or Aunt Grace who was a nurse in Green Bay and capable of wrestling a Green Bay drunk to the floor purportedly for medical purpose.

It was generally declared illegal to raise your feet above the top of the card table and the full-nelson also forbidden though a good ankle tackle was a beautiful thing to see in a farmhouse parlor. Experienced players rubbed Doctor Penwarren's Patent Bag Balm into their hands preventing opponents from getting the grip necessary to dislocate the fingers. Which is one of the reasons we let Aunt Grace play; she could pop a knuckle back into place quick as that.

Soon as a person gets four of a kind they go for a spoon, hoping not to attract attention. The contestants, trained to detect any sort of deviousness, are quicker than Wyatt Earp ever was, and the mad scramble is on as everyone lunges for the spoons. One strategem was to hold down your neighbor's hand while heaving your full body weight on the card table and so pin down all the spoons. The card table to this had been reinforced with 2 x 4 legs and the top underlaid by steel plate. The outward appearance of the contest at this point is the same huddle of bodies you see following a fumble in a football game, sans helmets, cleats and shoulder pads. Person was never sure what body part has pinned their face to the backside of their uncle's trousers. God help you if his dietary regimen had been anything but readily digestable starches. Neither was Aunt Grace the sort to back off 'cause she was a woman and sometimes Aunt Madge played and what with her perfume and padded bra a kid got educated as to the particulars in short order.

The hired man who wasn't otherwise worth two licks when it came to lugging feed bags was suddenly so inspired he lifted the table holding three uncles and my sister clean off the floor. Uncle Jim at ninety years though most ways dead was revived by the game, having the vigor and quickness of a fourteen notch gun-slinger and not about to get out-snatched by a young punk, meaning anyone under eighty. Uncle Jim used his cane to good advantage.

The cousins from Chicago thought they knew it all, having a union hall job at eight dollars an hour, felt obliged to teach their cousins a move or two. Course they never had their fingers dislocated before.

Every Christmas Pa rolled up the rugs and slid the good furniture into the spare bedroom. The portraits of the ancestors were unhitched from the wall, the lamps, end tables and drapes transported to the garage for safe-keeping. Mama's parlor as a result looked like a gaming pit missing only the straw to lay out injured animals. In the center stood the spoon table, around it a set of rummage sale chairs. We'd soon have kindling enough for the rest of the winter courtesy of those chairs. Nor did the spoons resemble spoons any more, this why my mama, hated Christmas.

Manure Pile

As a former purveyor of manure piles I have a certain lingering loyalty to midden heaps. As a farmchild I knew the special realm of that dimension. What the world saw as a gory pile of you-know-what was to my personal witness very nearly delicious in character. What kept my loyalty was the private passion... the non-nuclear fission a pile of manure invoked. Like nuke warheads, distinctive critical mass is required. I do not know what size is exact to the result but once a pile of manure gained a particular measure of superiority over the landscape, it began to heat up on the base of its own resolve. Not a mere esoteric heating but rapturous refractory heat, venting specialized gases and proud steam. Never did snow linger on the manure pile, no matter if the entire state of winter was snow-covered from Springfield to Fort York on the Hayes, that pile was clear and warm.

On a dark and wholly unkindled night in January a manure pile was the finest place ever to watch the sky. I have inspected many heavens, none better and more satisfying than what I beheld from the manure pile. The best position was to lay on it full-length and allow the heat to invade your whole person. Overcoming the initial squeamishness, a manure pile was a sort of advante

garde luxury. Freddie Hoyle never knew a better pinnacle to collect the night than a manure pile. I dreamed,
perhaps as all boys did then dream, of electrically heated
fleece-lined bomber suits of the kind worn in B-17's
24,000 feet over Nazi Germany. Fleece-lined from head
to toe and totally snow impervious, but equally unable
to move, much less think. I knew then the pious maxim,
to be comfortable is to give chance at the last measure of
thought without which a think is incomplete. Besides,
the manure pile needed nothing like fleece or World War
II at 24 volts to keep warm.

I did wonder what exactly was going on as could create warmth out of straw, cow dung and the occasional
placenta. Chemistry was right sinister stuff if plenitu-
dinous heat was to be had out of something as useless
as cow pies and yellow straw. No wonder folks went
into spasms over the terror of damnation and hell-fire
if a regular midden can stay off winter and boil snow.
Imagine what you could fire up with a pile of besotted
sinners, folks who were already warm to the touch.

What mystified me as that farmboy was how come
growed-ups didn't take a manure pile to its logical conclusion. Instead of burning infinite piles of wood, why
not heat the house with one enormous manure pile? The
raw product was at hand. The reason I figured dealt with
those things a kid ain't equipped to deal with. I simply
had to accept there was a good reason for not heating
houses with a natural farm by-product. Sometimes the
manure pile belched and ruminated, sending convulsions
and tremors through my backside. I sorta doubted the
wisdom of sitting a house smack atop a thing like that
but then it'd quit and act no more like Lady MacBeth and
I trust it again. By this time what the manure pile did
was of no matter, I had already lapsed into the specific
semiconscious ponder brought to fruit by a clear unwink-

ing winter night. A night immobilized at 28 below. The stars stooped from their saintly niches and hung just an arm length over my head. Stars came within the jurisdiction of the township, stars scraped against the fields and dislodged the fenceposts. Orion throwing his arm, climbed over the fence and sagged the wire... Orion in his long mane, his bare legs and kilt, whose long claymore hung bruised and dull from vanquishing fences. Followed after by barking Sirius, noisy white eyed Sirius lurching under the fencewire leaving a trail of dim hairy stars behind him.

I stared at Mars as if to conjure that planet and bring it closer to me. Else, it conjured me and I was taken by its red hand and pulled through the confining distance to see Mars as plainly as any field. Red sand and red dunes, a polar cap sixteen inches thick, maybe it was seventeen, of carbon dioxide that squeaked and hummed like carbon dioxide does, impatient to be gas.

Jupiter, I watched for moons, a game of sky walkers to find a moon without glass. The night must be earnestly still. The breath taken in and held as the gaze steadies and holds the poise till the thin light of Jovian moons squeaks by the over-inflated darkness.

It comes sooner or later, a change in the point of reference. I was no longer looking up but out. No longer the worshipful gazing to heaven but the farmer looking across his fields. That is all the difference, no more was to be had. The sky no longer above me but rather beyond, just across, beneath and beside. The perspective changes the boy. The earth no longer the second half of the sky but the merest porch-step from which to watch.

Maybe it was because I watched from the manure pile but all that emptiness, all those pitiless stars made me feel the more warmed than if I never watched the sky and never was lost in it. I don't blame people for not wanting to. A sky is antiseptic to the person, you leave your soul behind when you watch the sky in the still of a winter night. Turn back from your own gaze and you see yourself, there, smaller and smaller as the watch passes the rim of the galaxy. Then the nerve breaks and the eye is pulled back before it becomes lost in some avenue too far away to find its way back or care to.

A manure pile is admittedly a curious place to watch the winter night. From nowhere else was it clearer, nor the stars closer, or the darkness... so... warm... so exactly like the manure pile itself.

Moldy Hay

Any necromancer can testify that hauntings are conditional to their place of origin. A Norwegian ghost is not the same article as a Highland witch who in turn is not the least comparable to a vampire from Transylvania. All of whom when removed from their natural setting are not much of a ghost.

In like manner farmers are haunted by things that do not, cannot haunt a villager. A droughty summer or a cold wet August will spill more goblins, torture more nights in the township than the same stretch of bad weather within the city limits. It is this hypersensitivity to haunting that renders farmers susceptible to the creepy crawlies as accordingly miss the general public altogether. Of all the hallucinations applicable to farmers, the very worst is moldy hay. Cemetery ghost and taunting spirit have no better accomplice than hay as should have dried another day. Problem being of course every farmer commits the sin of moldy hay, out of desperation to fill the haymow with browse, out of anticipation of the weather, and because cattails and lily grass were not intended to be put in a hay bale in the first place.

Moldy hay comes in several models. The kind surest to cause haunting is low pasture hay, in actuality closer to a lily pond than a hay field. A place never intended by creation to ballast the haymow. Hay whose protein value is more from the corpse of smushed toad and baled garter snake than any worth of the fodder. To call the result hay is to propose feeding cows wood pulp and broomsticks. As said, desperation has everything to do with the onset of a good and woeful haunting.

The second ingredient to a proper metaphysical haunting is wanton behavior. This is why Norwegian ghosts are oft sighted singing Methodist hymns, as wanton an act as can be asked of a Norwegian spirit. A Scots goblin by the same rule is like to be seen drinking coffee. For farmers, making hay of bulrushes and tag alder is the sufficient insult to incur a haunting.

The third requirement is distaff architecture. You can not have ghosts without spooky castles, creaky stairs or cobwebby catacombs. Barns are excellent examples of this generally scary construction and old barns even better. Modern agriculture is an amalgamation of deserted farms conjoined under the banner of sheriff's auction and bankruptcy, in itself a swell inducement to a haunting specter whether or not the barn has been filled with quackgrass and cattails. The distaff and forlorn byre does not enjoy the same application of paint and window putty as does the primary barn and as result becomes the advertised menace to society. Whose id is to haunt farmers that there is here a roof to spare and they best fill it under with hay, surplus hay, if they are themselves to avoid the sheriff's cruel hammer. In this phantasm barn is piled away the hay from the bottom pasture better left to bobolinks.

The last, most vital ingredient of every haunting is personal injury; no ghost ever arrived at its station without suffering partial physical disintegration. Common routine injury simply will not do; stroke, AIDS, heartache, influenza, cancer do not a good ghost make. The occult is very specific on this issue, the injury must satisfy proper and rigid standards of gore. Such as Alistair MacNeil who married Adolf Oblewski's daughter who was Roman Catholic... that Alistair is now a ghost of legendary proportions in the township is due to the gruesome fate suffered by this ploughman. The community is divided whether the injury was from marrying a Catholic in the first place or because MacNeil died in a silo-filler. Died when his overalls caught and the silo-filler did what it was trained to do, the resulting funeral not of the open casket variety. In fact the lid was screwed down tight to prevent Widow NacNeil in a fit of grief from kissing Alistairs lips one last time, his lips being mixed with the tossed salad of his remains.

Had Alistair died in bed or in a car crash, his derelict barn on the marsh road might have passed into quaint obscurity. Going as he did in the more poignant manner resulted in the MacNeil barn becoming a centerpiece for the local occult. Dying in the silo-filler enthused the township's literary passions. Every farmhouse, every feed mill, every crossroad tavern and barbershop had a version of MacNeil's disjointed departure. Some even had what was rumored to be an official memento. Mementoes actually. The toe of Alistair in a jar of vinegar on the back wall of the Moore Barn tavern. Bobbing in the jar like a good toe ought. Found the morning after the coffin lid already screwed down tight. There was no way Alistair MacNeil's ghost could just plain retire to paradise with such manifold expectations on him. Not to mention the rumored bits and pieces of him hanging around neighborhood taverns. Which is fame of a sort you can't get without some mechanical advantage. Like a silo filler wound up to PTO speed and howling like a banshee as has gotten into the rhubarb wine. MacNeil's end to this juncture is however only interesting if we are curious into how many pieces a standard-size person can be rendered. While mathematically intriguing it is not particularly haunting, especially to farmers who are accustomed to being chewed up. Real haunting takes more than haphazard dismemberment. The ingredients must gel and coalesce properly.

What we have here are very good ingredients, now only to be well stirred and indecently marinated, and when altogether create a cosmic dose of the creepy crawlies. But to now add one late October night. A cold, marrow-chilling night. Add the essence of moldy hay. Add now the portent of that peculiar barn on that most peculiar back road that follows a crooked path through a very peculiar marsh. Stir into this Mister Alistar MacNeil, chopped into little pieces.

This author does not believe in ghosts, goblins or spirits, thinking them the product of lesser minds who are easy prey for the paranormal. That said, I will not traffic the road going past Widow MacNeil's barn any time after dark, knowing some neighbor filled the old barn with hay better left to kit fox and turtle. The very one where Alistair met his disassembling fate. And knowing as every farmer does moldy hay has one more as yet unmentioned attribute. Baling hay is one thing, baling willow bark and bobolink is another. Moldy hay is fermenting hay, it is warm and sweaty hay; it heats up, it pants, it respirates, it breathes. Forget Frankenstein. Moldy hay breathes a thousand breaths. A fog on a cool night is spawned of this breath. A fog indiscernible until the cold nacht of October. A tomb-scented fog that is both warm-blooded and sticky. A fog able to perambulate, to slink and crawl and hide behind trees. This the fog emanating from a derelict barn on a back road across the dark moor. Where once lived in one piece one Alistair MacNeil.

But this is only to suggest moldy hay is sorta creepy... what makes it truly scary is the sound. Moldy hay whimpers. The hay was too wet to bale. When fermentation started the twine holding the bales together reach a point where they kinda hum. A low eerie note. Barely audible. The bales having expanded torque the old barn beams. Wood grain grates against wood grain, the low almost growling sound can sometimes be felt in the ground for those are big barn beams. Alistair's haymow whines in an altogether and terrible chorus; a muttering, moaning dirge crudely mixed with whistles and whinnies. All this from a drear barn on a back road on the back end of October during the backside of the moon. Explanations from science for the behavior at this point are of no comfort.

.   .   .

On Halloween I would borrow my dad's pickup truck and load it with dubious friends, all of them doubters and heretics, village kids who didn't have any notion of moldy hay though they by now had heard the stories of Alistair. I'd take the town road which city folk find uncomfortable enough, much less when I switch roads below the second bridge taking the route across the marsh that slips ever so much further from the lights of village, then disappears completely into the obscuring murk. We cross the old plank bridge, a startling sound any time much less in the dark that moors have. The road to MacNeil's barn is on a tilt so I switch off the engine and let the truck drift eerily toward the foreboding bulk. Extinguish the headlights. All quiet except the crunch of gravel beneath the tires rolling suspiciously of their own accord. The barn seeming to rise from the ground, looming larger as we are drawn toward it. Closer. Closer. From a broken pane a wisp of fog is seen, a transmortal fog that acts alive. Another slithers at the cow door, a bank of the same creature straddles the road. My friends cease their glib banter when they smell the horrid, rank odor and how it seems to cling to the bumper and creep a ghastly severed hand over the tailgate. Then they hear for the first time the whimper of moldy hay. The very like heard from a gunny sack full of blind puppies in a drowning pail.

The conversion of heretics is a remarkable event. Doubters but an instant before, now screaming in unison as I hit the starter and spin the tires, and leave behind the lonesome spirits of MacNeil's barn.

I do not remember whether MacNeil's barn burned or just plain fell down. Widow MacNeil died in the nursing home a few years back so I guess there's no way to prove any of this happened the way I'm telling it. Which is the problem with ghosts and hauntings.

Like I said, I'm not inclined to believe in ghosts and such, but moldy hay is another thing.

Everything I Need to Know I Learned While Chasing Cows

I stole that line... the original says, everything I need to know I learned in kindergarten... written by a guy named Fulgam, Fulcrum, Folgers or something. Nice guy I guess, a macho jerk won't say things about kindergarten or what holding hands or a kitten does for a bad mood. Neither would a college professor or the local minister. Doesn't leave a lot of guys left who say nice things.

I went to a one-room school, it didn't have a kindergarten so I couldn't very well learn what I needed but I learned the stuff just the same. For me it happened while chasing cows to pasture... everything necessary and good I learned while chasing cows. I learned to examine the world, learned to be careful and watch where I was going. Learned to talk to God, to listen, to pee discreetly, to make my own noise if also discreetly.

Chasing cows was my first job. I knew it was a job because it fit all the definitions. Chasing cows every morning, following the same old rut, the same old hind ends. Before I knew it I had learned my first adult lesson... hating your job is obligatory.

I learned early on I wasn't paid enough. How's that for a major adult lesson? My salary at the time was a glass of Kool-Aid and fifteen cents a week, ten cents of which had to go in the collection plate at church leaving only a nickle a week for what economists call voluntary spending. Already I learned the economic facts of life — the things you want always cost more than you've got... Uncle Scrooge comic books were a dime, Bullseye Brand BBs ten cents a tube, the backhoe deluxe ice cream cone a dime too and cigars cost a quarter a box. I had a nickel and a nickel was only halfway to anything the least bit desirable. I learned another adult thing, saving. People with piggy banks get what they want, the rest make do with cheap thrills.

Every summer morning I chased cows. As a job it looked harder than it actually was, this again is widely applicable to adults. Most of the time the cows went by themselves and the only reason I chased them is so they wouldn't stretch the fence into Gilman's alfalfa.

I learned that jobs, all jobs, are a pain in the ass, meaning the only way to move the cows was address their vulnerable parts since you can't much reason with a cow. It is necessary to instruct the end of them as is willing to listen.

Once I let the cows go on down the lane while I busied myself at a bluejay nest. Soon enough the cows escaped into Gilman's alfalfa and I spent the most horrid morning trying to get them back, and even even horribler time explaining to my dad how such a thing happened.

I learned that explanations and excuses are the hardest kind of work there is in all the world. Not only did chasing cows save me from having to find a believable lie, it saved wear and tear on the fence and fixin' fence is also a lot harder work than chasing cows. To avoid fixing fence and a frantic search for excuses you better just chase the cows.

I learned a funny thing about work. What grown-ups call chores isn't the work itself as much as avoiding something worse. Chores are preventive maintenance — doing it now is usually better than cleaning up the consequences. Cheaper, too. I learned this applied to lots of stuff... like homework, 4-H projects, brushing teeth, painting, fixing the roof and cleaning the chicken coop.

I learned most jobs do not require a lot of intelligence, never mind any appearance that they do.

I used to worry about getting lost because the back pasture is so very far away you can't see it from here, but it's all a matter of following the path. Same as most jobs. Jobs have an end you can't see but you get there anyway if you only get started. Being afraid to start is the worst part. And I learned another thing... there is something worse than chores. Honest injun. Believe it or not there is something worse than work, it is having nothing to do. After all the rotten chores, all the crummy jobs, all the sweeping, the calf pens, there is something more awful and it is worklessness. I learned that work feels good.

I learned to sing while chasing cows and the cows don't mind whether I know all the words. Mostly I sang hymns though I had no idea what the words meant. Self-made noise is just like work, it feels good and no back pasture ever gave a hoot whether the pitch is right.

I learned that even though chasing cows is a pretty dumb job, stuff happens and if you don't watch out you'll step in it.

I learned that stuff washes off. No kiddin' — worst, gooiest, rottenest stuff you ever wanna mash your foot in... washes off. I learned that icky things are like that... except maybe tattoos and Mama won't let me get a tatoo like my Uncle Kingsley, who was in the Marine Corps. I learned not to get tattooed unless your mother says it's OK. If you do the tattoo, better say Mama.

I learned about gates. Not to open ones I wasn't strong enough to close. I can't figure out why it is there are gates a kid can open easy enough but once opened, take a tractor to get closed. I learned not to mess with anything you don't have the tools to fix.

I learned it is better to crawl under a fence than to go over the top unless your legs are real long.

I learned that barbed wire is a mean length of wire but it is the meanness that keeps the cows out of the neighbor's corn.

I learned that cows are pretty dumb and that the world is better off that way. It's the smart cows who kick.

I learned that cows are ladies and there are very few boy cows. I learned the essence of boy cows comes in a plastic tube and is administered by the guy with rubber gloves. I learned that boys are dangerous.

I learned not to eat blackberries until they are ripe. I learned not to follow anything too close.

I learned mud is great. Mud is to a kid what liquor is to a grown-up. July mud is the very best and going barefoot in mud is what heaven must feel like to the soul.

I learned good farm lanes have trees and badger holes and work is a lot better for having trees.

I learned that cows die. And calves die and the cats eat the gophers and that earthworms love the underside of stuff and that everything eats everything else. It's OK.

I learned there are people who don't want to talk about stuff or dying or look at it and never ever to touch it. I learned there is a big difference between what the cow lane teaches and what Sunday School teaches.

I learned the reason cows go to pasture willingly is because in the morning it seems a better place than the barn because of green grass and lots of shade and a stream at the low end. But by the end of the day the barn looks better again and they go home. I learned life is like that.

Farm Games

The spring in Wisconsin is conducted like a public execution. The victim, who has been locked up for a long time, is dramatically hauled out into broad daylight and summarily reduced to their essences. This is the purpose of northern spring, to acquaint us again with our essences.

Spring for unknown reasons sometimes raises the temperature to tropical levels and what was snow-covered a moment before is immediately after water-logged. Being Central Wisconsin is flatter than a barn cat killed on a blacktop road in July by an eighteen wheeler carrying a bulldozer, when snow melts of that sudden tropic, and the ground still frozen, the water ain't got nowhere to go. The place being flat, water doesn't flow as much as ooze one direction or another.

The farm fields are transformed into a shallow lakes anywhere from a quarter mile wide to something near oceanic. A foot deep, maybe two. Like as not these seas straddle roadways, also inundate and submerge, as a result stranding farms in isolated principalities that can neither be rescued nor escaped. Coincidentally, such a melt precludes almost every known chore on the farmstead save the most rudimentary.

It is a known fact of human behavior that, given a

surplus of resource and an excess of liberty, a sport will be made of it. So it happened between an assortment of neighbor kids we created what we thought resembled the Great Armada. The sport being to manufacture from junk wood a craft that, with a stout pole, was propelled across this oceanic expanse. The rules of construction closely followed those of the America's Cup: no engines, only sails and lumber (ours was junk lumber), no parents, figureheads required.

Just like the America's Cup, we immediately set to cheating. My next door neighbor Tom had found a real rowboat oar, and our cousin Mark visiting from Rhinelander and was now marooned, had the audacity of asking our dad for a box of nails to build his boat. Our dad actually gave him a four pound box of brand new nails, as wasn't in accord with the generally accepted rules. When we had to gain ours from the supply in the milk can in the corner of the farm shop, besides straightening them out.

Each contestant was allowed one day to build the craft, the contest to follow the next afternoon, like as not a Sunday and since the roads were flooded, we couldn't kirk. We lined up the boats on one side of an as-yet-uncrossed expanse of water. In the beginning the simple object was to reach the far shore. We soon learned this wasn't that much of a contest, in fact nothing more than a drag race when what we were after was something closer to the 24 hour de Le Mans, meaning a classic marathon. To this end we drew up a more compelling course. After crossing the first puddle, we were to drag our craft across the penninsula to relaunch it in the next body of water, overland again to a third open sea, follow there the tree line which was more or less dry land to a final expanse of watery grave abutting the town road and then the last half mile to the finish line. The circumference of this rough circle, a distance of about three nautical miles, not that any of us knew what a nautical mile was but it sounded appropriate and dangerous.

Our cousin from Rhinelander also broke the rules about new boards, using lumber from the pile that would have gotten us killed had we touched it. As a result his craft had a slim appearance while to ours were more rumination than actual buoyancy. We were not however distressed, noting our cousin, who was a generous measure of kid, just happened to pick black oak lumber for his ship.

The rest of the fleet was composed of what had in a former life been roof boards, desk tops, doors, and potato boxes that looked perfectly awful in the guise of a boat, but by happy coincidence was as buoyant as a Spanish cork. Jimmy S., always more inventive than the rest of us, had made his boat out of a refrigerator box that he overlaid with several coats of varnish rendering it, theoretically, insoluble. It was an instant marvel for it floated like a thistle seed, if still looking very much like a refrigerator box.

Our start gun was a whole roll of caps placed at the bottom of a piece of pipe that when hit dead on with a rock, exited from the open end with a cannon-like bellow over the semi aquatic expanse. The race was on. Our cousin from Rhinelander immediately took the lead with his sleek illegal craft and was already across to the second sea before the rest of us were halfway across the first. Jimmy S. discovered guidance problems with the refrigerator box, finally cut out a hole in one end so he could lay down and pole the boat forward from a prone position. Using this stance, he recovered admirally. The rest of us just sorta stirred. I became so desparate for velocity that I jumped in the water entire and pushed the boat, actually a former barn door, in the desired direction.

"Foul," shouted my cousin from Rhinelander who had what he believed an insurmountable lead. My younger brother, the one who would go on to law school, saw the portent of pushing the boat through the water but did not, as is the case with lawyers, anticipate the cold.

The cousin from Rhinelander did in the end win the race, though we made him sweat it. Jimmy S's cardboard boat began taking on water by the return leg up the South Atlantic. The cousin had his worst moment coming around the Horn, this the fenceline where he should have stayed close to the fence where the ground was hard. He went wide, as a result sunk to his waist in mud that sucked at him so loud we could hear it slurping at him between his squeals. Luckily the boat was a wide pile of trash for the quickmud to swallow and that saved him.

Like I said, our cousin won. He immediately went for the house and told our mother how he needed a warm bath. We had chores to do, so chucked our wet clothes in the mud room, threw a pair of dad's overalls over our nakedness and went to the evening milking. It was after all, spring.

The Neighbor's
Junk Pile

The neighbor's junk pile was to the township what is now provided by the National Enquirer and the Playboy Channel. Every farmer had one, a junk pile that is, and a couple times a year the kids took a loaded wagon to it and added another layer.

Most farms had two junk piles; repository number one and repository number two. Repository number one was the preliminary junk pile just behind the shed. It wasn't a junk pile as much as a mediation pile. The accumulates were only half-way junk, not absolutely junk. Less a junk pile than something of a reference library.

My father stored third degree junk in the repository number two. Second degree junk was stored in the pile behind the shop and first degree junk huddled in a semi-fluid state beneath the workbench. Doesn't take an archeologist to discern each of these accumulations had a reference point in the human scale. The definition of the first degree junk found under the workbench is that it might fit some agricultural impliment yet current. Second degree junk would fit if some modified; third degree junk wasn't useless as much as the current generation didn't recognize the pieces any more. After that, it was junk and went to the woods.

Once farmers kept woods as an act of self-defense. Not only did the woodlot protect the farm from wind, it offered a contribution to his winter survival. The ultimate worth of the woods was a place to conceal household and farmstead junk. Junk was an intimate thing for farmers, who liked nothing better on a rainy afternoon, under the guise of chasing heifers, than to sneak over the fence and inspect their neighbor's junk pile. Notice what sort of bottles were they throwing away. Did they eat canned beans or was there a surplus of chipped mason jars, a telling reference to the lady of the house, who could or couldn't cook. Which wasn't always apparent at the church supper since the food was intentionally shuffled to prevent open warfare between those who could cook, and those the Lord had not so favored.

Neighbors knew this, knew their otherwise friendly kinsmen down the road were, when the lights went off, nothing but a bunch of dirty rotten window peepers. Meaning junk pile lookers. They knew for certain because when they had the chance, they did the same. There were few things so erotic as spying on the neighbor's junk heap.

This is why the junk pile went through several per-mentations before the stuff finally got hauled off to the woods. It is the very same method used by the War De-partment, who went to the trouble of declassifying mili-tary secrets before dumping the remains in a deep ocean trench. Among farmers, the really incriminating stuff was burnt before it got hauled off to the junk pile. Never mind a brandy bottle is still a brandy bottle unless you bust it, and even then the bottle neck has a guilty look.

As a kid I loved our neighbors' junk piles, I knew where every one was no matter how diligent their effort to hide it. I was less interested in analyzing their junk and tallying up any private sins represented by bought pie filling and canned tomatoes, as a quiet afternoon with glass bottles, me and my bolt action single-shot. I did not then recognize I was a primary agent in a geological process that pulverized solid waste into a more digestable form. At the time I believed nothing on earth died with the zest of a glass bottle, unless of course you happen to have some live grenades. What was middlin' nifty was to fill a bottle with a little gasoline, place a lighted candle underneath and blast away from fifty yards.

What I didn't shoot at, I pryed apart in search of a trophy, a nice lens or a piece of chain. When I went to the neighbor's woods I carried with me a burlap sack to carry home the more interesting bits. So interesting were the items in the neighbor's junk pile that instead of the pile accumulating, it actually receeded. The wagon load secreted to it in April was totally reabsorbed into the township by the end of July.

Besides a .22 caliber rifle, I carried a pair of vice grips, screw driver and crescent wrench in my pocket, and two gunny sacks. It was amazing what had at last defined itself as junk on the neighbor's farmstead proved vital stuff next door. I dragged home headlights, vaccuum tubes, magazines, catalogs, hinges, lamps, wheels of every kind, defunct toasters, hammer heads, backless chairs, radiator caps, spark plugs, old shingles, license plates, dash boards, frayed suitcases, stub pencils, typewriters frozen in utterance, hubcaps... those were the glory days of chrome plated hubcaps, buxom, warrior-queen hub-caps with DeSoto blazoned across the equator. I revelled in all engine parts, collecting pistons and crankshafts, connecting rods and true brass carburetors. In my shack I was building a 12-cylinder engine with two thousand horsepower and I'd never have to pitch manure or silage again, just start that engine and let its prop wash fulfill the crummier chores.

There was in the township in those days a thin layer of farmkids picking over junk piles, what went out by wagonload came back by the sack. Nobody thought landfills were the least bit necessary; but that was before TV dinners and the whole point of having a mama in the first place was to avoid unnecessarily junking up the woods with store-bought.

I believe there is a statute against a junk pile in the woodlot. I am comfortable with that, this is, after all, the disposable age. Besides, there are not enough farmkids any more to render junk a complete ecosystem. Still, I am of that other age, when another farmer's scrap pile looked like a treasure, and when I had the chance, I was happy to escort it home.

Cosmology, physics and the Bible are undecided, whether Genesis began from nothing, or otherwise. I have no such doubt, believing as I do in the junk pile. Junk presages every thing. Before an item becomes a collectable it must first endure a period of being plain junk. What was once moldering in an ancient midden is now a hushed museum exhibit. What this proves is obvious... in the end there ain't no such thing as junk, and no end neither.

Literacy and my Mama's Linoleum

I learned to read because my mama put words on the floor. Every afternoon she put words on the floor. In the spring at mud-time she increased the dosage.

My mama had this affliction, the mop bucket and words; she could not use the one without deploying the other. Every afternoon the kitchen, the dining room, the bathroom got a slathering from the mop, followed after by a layer of newsprint.

We rarely ever saw the floor. It was linoleum though I'm not quite sure. Coulda been alabaster with inlaid nubian figurines, though I think it was linoleum, roll linoleum. The kind they don't sell any more 'cause nobody would put what amounted to roofing paper on a floor. Federal law now prevents its use in a house where children are present, because it is capable of refrigerating the floor to a temperature experienced in Antarctica. As a child I did not visit the bathroom at night, I did not go for a drink of water, I did not raid the cookie jar, I did not venture out of bed because that linoleum floor was in the way. Even in mid-July you could frostbite your toes on that stretch of linoleum any time after dark. Our house didn't need a refrigerator, we had a linoleum floor.

As did the very same thing and didn't require plugging into the wall.

My mama was proud of her linoleum, the way a farm woman might be who lives at a distance from civilizing factors. My mama thought highly of her linoleum. It was genuine storebought. If you looked close you could decipher in it a kind of floral pattern, least my mama could.

There was nothing on earth Mama hated more than for her floor to get trashed by a bunch of wild Indians trapsing mud and cow stuff over her shiny storebought. So every afternoon she mopped the floor and covered it with newspaper. The entire east end of the house was a layer of newspaper. A layer that, like as not, lingered to the next day, at which time the floor was mopped again and yesterday's newspaper applied.

I do not think as a child I was inclined to literacy more than any other kid. Left to my own prerogatives I would have been entirely satisfied to continue my existence in the semi-barbaric phase. And would have, but for the accident of my mama mopping her linoleum floor every day, followed by an ointment of newsprint.

The average newspaper is by itself an uninteresting specimen, it has almost no natural appeal. But disembowel and spread it like fillets of fish sun-drying in an Eskimo village, and this same dull device becomes interesting. The very same phenomenon works in the bathroom while sitting on the device. Take any dry, over-wordy, prevaricating, technically inept writing, also Shakespeare, something in Sanskrit, that Irish madman James Joyce, an essay of Emerson, a Russian novel, the obitury column from farther Topeka, lay it on the floor and it becomes... interesting. No sooner had Mama mopped the floor than crossing the dining room or kitchen could no longer be done at a single stride. Three paces into the transit and the voyager was brought to their knees by something interesting on the floor.

There were evenings when every member of the household was on the floor, elbows to our chins, reading the newspaper.

I have come to think, that the acquisition of literacy requires a requisite tension. As a kid I do not once recall reading the newspaper while sitting in a chair, but thrown on the floor, put underfoot, that white mass of newsprint was so very inviting. To this day I do not know why.

Currently my house is breaking to manners two puppies, foundlings who by chance replaced a mongrel springer. To render them hospitable, these dogs have to learn to control themselves and their digestive tract. To this education are newspapers deployed. The spring season being busy, I have not had much time to give the paper more than a passing glance, except those pages featured prominently on the floor.

How dull is a headline while sitting in a chair. It is not the same banner when lying spreadeagled on the bathroom floor.

I remember once having the stomach flu. My mama came into the room and, seeing me, uttered something darling and sweet (unusual for a farm mother), for my pose was of the very ill, head hanging over the edge waiting to upchuck. In reality I was reading the newspaper because it was there, lying on the floor.

Were I a school administrator I would throw out all the textbooks, bulldoze holes in the walls of the classrooms, tear out the tiled floors, get several thousand mop pails, rag mops also and a thousand linear feet of old fashioned linoleum flooring. I would mop the floor every morning and afternoon, then spread across this damp surface a layer of newsprint, inclusive of MacBeth, the formulas of analytic chemistry, diagrams of sentences, Latin phrases, history of ancient Rome, the Greek alphabet... and then allow the student population to freely graze over this expanse.

To prove the validity of the method I would install over this same assembly a battery of televisions, video terminals and arcade games spilling out every pop, bop and fizz known to inhabit the cathode ray tube. My bet is the kids, however lowly their origin, including farmkids, would be on their knees soon, and ever after. Compelled to read by a force of nature likened to gravity, only better.

Marsh Child

My affection for the Buena Vista Marsh began as a child, it was that even a child could see and know the difference of the place. If the highland fields of the farm were mellow with alfalfa and potatoes and the woods there were good oak and sweet maple, the marsh was otherwise. The highland was a mineral soil, sandy loam if some more sand than loam; the marsh was here too otherwise. The marsh was muck, a strange name for a soil and it a strange soil. It seemed rendered of old mattresses, the marsh ground jiggled, it sighed and it wasn't very nice to alfalfa. Its woods too were of another sort, here grew tamarack and balsam fir, cedar and tag alder, basswood, aspen, birch, paper, silver, yellow. Here fused forth stray expulsions of red-bark, was said that Indian tobacco kinnicannic was a mix of red-bark, willow leaf and sumac. As a child I smoked pipes fashioned of plumbing fixtures stoked with kinnicanic and found it nice enough but not so much as to form a good habit.

On the matter of life the marsh seemed a different enthusiasm, it was refuge to all things, badgers were at home on the sandy dunes and stream berms, snakes, frogs, fox, coyotes, deer, hawks, falcon, ducks, owls, even bear were sighted in routine. As soon as one crossed that line separating the low dominion from the highland earth there was a physical difference, a different feel to the very air, kingdom and phylum were different, trees and smells were different. Only the sky was the same and sometimes not even that.

A mile below our house on the town road was the first of many bridges, eight altogether between the farm house and the next village of Bancroft, these bridges spanning the drainage ditches of the Buena Vista Marsh. West were more bridges over more ditches. As children we formed secret clans that met at chosen occasions, mostly Sunday afternoons, under these bridges. Here we burned solemn fires of birch and tamarack and shared choice pages from the ladies undergarment section of the Monkey Ward catalog. I don't know why the elastic girdle held such an attraction for us, probably for the same reason a bear or wolverine was an attraction, because they were so seldom seen. Sometimes the very rumor of strangeness is enough to inspire a kid to go look for it.

We had heard the stories, stories of the marsh. Stories of Indians and wolves, bootleggers, whisky stills, quicksand, loggers, farm equipment and amputees. Strange things it seemed happened on the marsh. We had seen with our very eyes the wondrous and slightly discomforting bridge of John Eckels, Civil War veteran John Eckels and his creosote wonder. The bridge you see went nowhere but in whose under-beams were more trout than a decent universe should hold in one place; so we swam with trout as not every kid can say. Brook trout speckled and fiery when the beams of light caught them and they exploded. Super novas, black holes, neutron stars, brown dwarfs, spiral galaxies, all of these caught in the vortex of that abridge, the one going nowhere. We watch a universe at birth under that bridge while swimming with trout. We blended in this cold stew with the mind and soul of trout, of the birds, too, the trees, the ghosts of wandering Winnebago. By cold water immersion were we bestowed the other gospel, the marsh testament, the Marsh Version not the King James, where worth was measured in trout, trout equal to corn and gravel roads, trout equal to power lines and new cars, trout equal even to Sunday School. Our baptism here was by the other god, to another creation, who loves man no better than the trout, in whose image he is not, except where the image is of them together. We were children when we found this to be so, there on the marsh, it was a scary thing to know. This then was our clan, our root of belonging, this why the marsh was then and yet on the back side of the farm. From whence we heard the sounds and cries of all times, of wolf and condor, saber tooth, Druid and Winnebago, all of them yet alive and comforted by the marsh.

On the farm were five or six miles of stream edge, seeps, stream bank, springs, trickles, boggings, cow killers. Burns, our grandfather called these streams. Some he called bravlies, a word for a merry little stream. He had a hundred different words for stream and creek. A bushie was overgrown, a fallkirk was noisy, a babblin' less noisy than a fallkirk, a dramer was little noticed water, a sippin' he called it, a burn was good enough for tea.

I was baptized by waters, a thousand times baptized was I. I heard water tell its stories, I slept nights by it, comforted. I saw its birds, fabulous and jeweled. I was cooled there, it my Eden, it beckoned me to return to nakedness and animal joy. Here I ran with the deer and the cows on moonlit nights, naked but for moccasins. I ate my bologna sandwich lunch with pickles on hot summer days while mowing, my soul woven to this place. I had seen its ghosts and heard their side, some in language unknown. I wooed my woman here, among the seeps and wigglies, the cressinks and the beast pools, among the man-takers and murder holes. That being an old

spring hole whose bed of soft muck, if probed with a
long stick seems to possess no bottom. Here a weighted
body can hide a thousand years and none the wiser but
for a few methane-rich bubblings, this why they are called
murder holes.

At some point I knew my totem, and it was trout,
cold-willed and sleek, brook trout more than brown. As
I was baptized by waters so was I baptized by trout and
the place of them. Less did I come to fish than watch, this
the mark of a burn bairn, less to hunt as to watch. To this
day I am a lousy fisher, I bumble about, I snare trees, the
fly disobeys, but yet can I sit on the waterlogged stump
and visit with my kinfolk. How pleasant the early winter
afternoon spent with them, their terrible orange bellies
engaged with fire, like shards broken off the dawn sky
and now wildly spilled in the waters. Here in the marsh
and low woods is my glass temple, my marble-floored
cathedral.

I can admit this now, though it was the child who was
baptized and made the marsh variant. I can now say it
serves as well as the advertised brand. I have one simple
conscience, to keep marshes, to keep waters. I will not
say humankind is better or kinder for this, only that cold
running water makes for a different kind of bone.

Farmboys as Lovers

I was once afraid of sex. The correct expression is paranormal fear. If you don't believe me, ask my wife. She will tell you when we dated I was out-classed by urban males. I wasn't even on the same lap as those guys, not even on the same race track. When it comes to successful replication, this is not a good beginning.

The reason I feared sex and its consequences is because I was a farmkid. Lore has it that farmkids know all about the birds and the bees, also about dogs, cats and salamanders. How this is supposed to prove an advantage to a kid, I still don't know. In particular, I was a farmkid attached to the kingdom of the milk cow. I can't offer any opinion on what relationship kids had to sex who weren't raised on dairy farms; they might have been more liberated. They might have been knowledgable and suave and knew all the wrestling holds and how to undo harness buckles single-handed. My wife says there were guys at her high school who could do this from three rows back, so very good were they.

Kids raised on a potato farm were different. I remember them as fearless. It was mostly Catholics who raised potatoes in the former farm epoch, because they alone had kids enough to pick them; it was the Catholic farmboys who were fearless. The reason is because the potato didn't kick the same way a milk cow can kick. Potatoes might screw you over and send you back to the bank to ask for more money, but they didn't kick your actual teeth down your throat, even though it sometimes felt like it.

I have been kicked every way loose by a milk cow. Which explains why there is nobody on earth with more respect for the female than a farmkid raised on a dairy farm. It is a nearly divine education, of exactly how and where to put your hands on another creature's anatomy and not get your teeth served for lunch. Some profess what is involved is a matter of technique. Technique, they say. Those who say this have never laid their hands on the soft flesh of a strange female for the purpose of gratifying a milk pail. Technique alone will get you killed, particularly when the lady in question is some sixteen hundred pounds heavier than you are. Imagine please, the extreme and lethal nature of this romance with a re-quest is so kinky as to involve a stainless steel machine capable of 15 pounds negative thrust.

There is on earth no sweeter mouth than the farmkid about to perform the act of the evening lactation on a blue-eyed female with cute ears. Technique alone would get them killed. The only venue remaining is sweet-talk. And this, uttered to a female who does not recognize Shakespeare's sonnets as the greatest love poems ever written. In fact, a female who does not understand Eng-lish, nor French, nor Gaelic, nor old Sumarian, but does understand the primordial and universal soothe. Who is disarmed, if the noise is sufficiently calming.

As a farmkid I learned to speak the very same language spoken in the Garden of Eden. That former and famous language rumored to exist in the perfect interval, before Eve arrived, followed not long after by the snake in the red convertible. Where for the briefest moment, Adam spoke to the animals and they understood. The language used wasn't hippopotamus or hawk, neither dolphin, muskrat or rattlesnake; it was the language of all of them, a language without harsh consonants and where vowels didn't hang precariously. It was almost Shakespearean, if a little better because even the lizards in the back row understood. White deer and elephants understood. This language flowed like water, it was mellow and rather habit-forming because you could speak with animals, some of whom went on to become milk cows.

I do not know how I learned to speak with animals. My father insisted it couldn't be taught, that it was something I would have to learn by myself. When I protested I was not old enough to touch females so intimately, he suggested I hurry up and learn. Was then he handed me a 30-pound Surge milker, a surcingle and pointed out the next cow in line. Speak to her, he said. Gain her confidence. At least open the discussion.

I believe milking cows when you're a kid makes a difference on a person. People who have not milked cows ought not attempt dangerous things with words. Knowing this I have rather different qualifications for the presidential candidates than have my fellow Americans. If the prospective office-seeker can not put the rigging pin back into a hand grenade by talking at it, they best be advised not to attempt milking a sixteen hundred pound lady. If they can not close a pasture gate by power of words, best not attempt intimacy with a well-endowed and well-heeled blue-eyed Babe. And if they would please not bother the Oval Office, that would be nice, too.

It might be thought that any farmkid who survives this task would be a most fluent adult. This might be true, had every attempt been met with equal receptivity. Fluency in the tongue of angels and milk cows does not come so easy. A nice batting average is the best you can hope for, but fluency is something else. Milk cows are that proud, and sometimes it seems just want to knock that little sucker out of the park. Just when you think you're good, real good, just when you think you're cool as a cucumber sandwich served under boxelders... suddenly there is that bird's-eye view of everything. Always the need then to search out another behavior-modifying sonnet to whisper to the ear, and such a lovely ear it is, of this darling, this dappled holstein heifer third stanchion over.

Some say farmboys are the best lovers, because they know how to handle dumb beasts.

Some say farmboys are lousy lovers, because they are tired of saying loving things by the time they get in from the barn.

It's not for me to offer an opinion.

The Particulars
of Pup Tents

When I was a pup to an alligator, the full expression of my courage was to go tenting at the far end of the cow pasture. My hope was what might, during the dark and pitiless portion of the night, think me edible, would find the cows with whom I shared the pasture more so. Edible that is. Besides, I was smarter than a cow. Any monster as ate me was in for a terrible stomach ache since I hadn't taken off my clothes. My shoes neither. Besides which I had filled my pockets with pole nails to render myself less succulent than milk cows.

Was in the back pasture our parents allowed us to have fire. We could sleep under the apple trees if we wanted but we couldn't tend fire there. Too close to the house, they said. Our mama didn't trust what fool thing we might set fire to, such as tarpaper, wheelbarrow tires and old fence posts that spit off sparks the size of dog houses. This didn't bother us, but it bothered our mama.

Hence the rule about fire in the apple tree orchard. In the cow pasture our mama didn't care, more importantly, she didn't know. It was there we learned the fundamentals of fire and fire-tending, and that a good pan of raw fries can be cooked over a burning tire. Though the French already knew this.

The image that haunts me yet is of my grandfather visiting our camp one night. Him and Uncle Curtis heard we were camping on the back-end of the pasture and them two wandered out, bearing Oreo cookies and a couple gallons of cold milk. They hadn't even sat down before Grandpa Eugene was complaining about the paucity of our campsite, 'cause it didn't have the right furniture. Him and Uncle Curtis wandered off into the dark and a few minutes later came huffing back into the light of the campfire dragging the most-wise share of a desiccated pine tree. They drew this close up by the fire, jockeyed it back and forth same as our mama would to situate a davenport. At last satisfied, they flopped down and leaned back in an attitude of Roman imperial decadence.

I can yet see that image of my grandfather. The way the fire lit him, his long sleeved shirt, his suspenders, his rumpled fedora, the reflection of the fire from his plain round eyeglasses. Behind him was our pale canvas tent, standing like a white wedge against the dark deep of the night.

He was in his seventies at the time he came to our campsite, but he sat there, like us, the same mesmerized look on his face. A man of seventy years, still mesmerized by a fence post and corn stubble campfire, is a thing to see.

The image of him; old, wise, some parts bitten off, and watching the fire, the same as us. I remember that look of a grown man so like a child, looking into fire. On his face the look of the whole crayon box, all its colorations. Wonder. Contentment. Pleasure. Nurture. Peace. Bliss. Contentment. Satisfaction.

Was that look on my grandfather's face that haunts me to this day; there is a reason it should. Because the elements that made that look possible will never happen for most people, not even once in their lives. What are those elements? They are simple enough. One grandfather or an approximation of that. Some kids. Again easy enough to come by. A campfire. Easy at least for some kids. For those who need most the counsel of a campfire, this is only a remote possibility. The last element is, alas, quite, quite rare… a pup tent. Lots of places still have campfires but not many have pup tent campfires. There is a difference between fires. True, there is fire in a stove and fireplace and fire in a charcoal grill. But a pup tent campfire is different and it isn't the burning wheelbarrow tire that makes it so. The difference is vulnerability. The flimsy tent changes everything. Substitute a camper or a cottage by the lake, and the elements of that crayon box are scattered, the colors are pale and less varied. Fragility is the thing, what only a pup tent can achieve. This and the distance from the house multiplied by the specific gravity of the darkness.

He haunts me, my grandfather, leaning to the fire, in his eyeglass two miniature fires, a two day growth of beard on his face, that pale tent behind, the luxuriant dead tree at his back reflecting the warmth of the fire. No campsite should ever be without a consummate length of dead tree.

Framing this picture is the darkness. If only the world would believe in such darkness again. Like a hatch cover was that darkness, screwed down tight and gasketed… was that darkness. A darkness so deep, the far end of a cow pasture is a lot farther off than you'd suppose.

That is what I remember. His glasses glinting, two Oreos in his right hand, milk on his lip. "Let me tell you of Sotuskongah," he said, "he of the Winnebago …"

The Jackknife

My uncle gave me my first jackknife and was my mama pissed. It was Christmas, I was seven; Mama thought I was too young. I thought the knife overdue.

Uncle Curtis never married and farmed his entire and well-done life in Valley Up. I have since regreted that Uncle Curtis didn't marry and have kids. 'Course if he had, his kids would have gotten the farm and not his sister's kids which is where I came in.

Uncle Curtis was not particular good with kids, his manner was gruff, short, ill-tempered, like he didn't want to be bothered with us following after. Why we did follow him I don't know, but we did. Not being married and not having kids of his own, Uncle Curtis had none of the reticence about doing weird and physical-injury type stuff that fearing parents wouldn't allow if they had known. We all knew how vitally important it was to keep parents uninformed.

Like the time Uncle Curtis hitched the mow fork to a hay bale and let us ride it to the peak of the barn, where the fork hit the track and ran like a horse on fire to the far end of the barn. Where the fork released and dropped whoever was riding it about 15 feet into the mow of loose straw. From this most delicious plummet we dragged the bale back to Uncle for to do the thing all over again. My mistake was telling Mama how much better this was than the Ferris Wheel at the Amherst Fair and better even than the Bullet which I wasn't allowed to ride anyway. I learned not to relate every good thing and emotion to my mama.

The jackknife was a cheap thing with a genuine tin almost bone handle that fell off. Didn't matter. I thought the knife looked the more savage with the bare brass frame and blades. I was ten before my mama thought I was old enough for a jackknife despite by this time Uncle Curtis at Christmas and birthdays had given me half a dozen cheap good for nothing jackknives. He knew they would get lost.

I felt like a person is supposed to feel about a knife, like I was going on naked if there wasn't a jackknife in my pocket. I learned you could pass the most boring job in the world if you had the jackknife on your person; nothing relieved boredom and pestilence better than a jackknife. Whittling is a most comforting motion. It has no more purpose than chewing gum or playing pool but it made waiting for the stock tank to fill a good job. So was waiting for the next wagon to fill with oats or hay or straw or potatoes. What a jackknife might have conferred on the Sunday morning sermon I can hardly imagine without sounding sacrilegious. Not that I could see any difference between whittling during the sermon and what Mrs. Coleman did. She knit the whole while, except at the prayers, and even then I could see her fingers twitch. I didn't see the difference myself. So maybe she was knitting mittens for orphans in Kenya, it is way too warm in Kenya for mittens anyway. My thought was they'd appreciate dry shavings same as did my grandfather, dry shavings every morning for the kitchen stove.

At seven years old, with a jackknife in my pocket, I felt equipped … I mean Eeeequipped. I seen my dad gap a spark plug with his jackknife, clean his fingernails, scrape paint, dig out a sliver, tighten a screw, hammer in a tack, adjust a float, cut a rope, trim a board, splice a wire, cut the top off a can of roofing tar, clean his teeth, ream out a glue hole and it wasn't yet dinner time.

I had the sense I could survive just about anywhere save Saudi Arabia if I had a jackknife in my pocket. If the car ever went off the bridge into McDill Pond I could cut a hole in the roof and escape. I have no idea why I thought this might prove necessary but I did.

My dad scraped the inner tube for the patch with his jackknife despite they included a scraper with every box of Monkey Patches. He whisked back the dirt in the corn rows to check the seed set. With his jackknife he scraped away the paint for the ground clamp of the welder, pried open a stuck silo hatch, cleaned trout at the creek, and tossed it at the ground in a sort of absent minded game when the salesman from the feedmill proved long-winded. A sign for the guy to quit talking and leave. He opened bags of bran and seed corn and fertilizer, made a toothpick, dissected a bug, and cut cow manure into little slices looking for a wonderful kind of worm. He did this with his jackknife. Once when straightening the lightning rod on the barn ridge, his foot slipped and put him in proximity of taking the short cut to the ground. My dad drove his jackknife into the roof and hung on like Hillary on Everest; being wise he never told Mama. He marked the length of a board he wanted to cut using his jackknife, cut away afterbirth, that afternoon he used the same knife to cut the birthday cake when Mama forgot to bring a knife to the field and wanted to surprise him. Didn't tell Mama about that neither. Myself, I thought the cake tasted the better for the experience.

When my dad died, before they closed the box, I snuck a jackknife in his pocket. I kept his old one and let him have my new Swiss Army. I can get another knife.

Rodeo

I do not understand rodeos. They may advertise themselves as cowboy events but I know better. The awful truth is cowboys aren't real... cowboys. They may say they are, but it's a dash-burn falsification, besides a damnable lie, that... cowboys are cowboys. Horseboys maybe, floppy-hat, cactus-jumping, saddle-sore, prairie lads maybe. But cowboys? Not on your life are the sunburned oysters on those long legged kangaroos ... cowboys.

I know this for an absolute fact.

Flat-dab-gum-honest-to-Alacazam fact.

A holy-Jesus-mother-mama-Jeremiah-Jacob... fact.

They ain't cowboys, nobody in Texas is. Colorado neither. Nobody wearing one of those high plains umbrellas on their head... is a cowboy.

This I know.

Absolute.

Genuine.

'Cause,

I was.

A cowboy.

Once.

I mean a COW-boy.

Which brings me back to rodeo.

Once when we were no bigger than wire nails on a beanpole, we decided to have ourselves a rodeo. An out-behind-the-barn kind of rodeo. A where-mama-can't-see-yah kind of rodeo. We took one of the tamer cows from the barn, rigged a kind of hang-on device around her middle, squeezed her up next to the fence where one of our membership got on.

I have two brothers; one of us rode that cow that day. One of us got shook off with such howitzer spectacle, if we'd had a video camera, we'd still be hog-deep into the residuals and reruns of that image. One of us landed in a mush the human body isn't designed for, smacked the better part of their brain clear back to the dinosaur and ain't been able to think clear sequential thoughts ever since. Being brothers, we protected the identity of the victim. Being farmers, the lack of brain function has never been any particular disadvantage.

Eventually our dad discovered the unnatural thing we did to one of his cows. Truth is, he found out that very evening. The cow blabbed. Told our dad we tried to have a rodeo on her back. Not in so many words did this cow tell our dad, was the way she acted. Same skittered, cross-eyed behavior as happened on a maiden aunt who once wandered into an adult magazine store, who came out blinking her eyes that same dull way, as if a grenade had gone off under her pillow. In no uncertain terms we were told never to again appropriate milk cows for purposes of a rodeo. Try a heifer if we wanted, but leave the milk cows alone.

Nowadays, if a father said to his precious children what our father said to us, they'd have him in handcuffs so fast his nose hairs'd fall out. It was not only abusive, what our father said to us, it was facilitating. He ought not have done that, being we already were down to two normal brain functions out of a possible three, and on our way to farther erosion.

Ride a heifer, huh?

Real rodeo, for real cowboys, is not about grown men riding skinny, semi-transparent range cows. Real rodeo is what happens when you put a 91-pound barnkid on a well nourished holstein. The power to weight ratio of average cow vehemence is twelve to one. The same effect as driving a V-12 Testa Rosa Ferrari with one hand on the steering wheel and the other under the fan belt where it goes around the generator. What you have here is linear sensation without any detours. Horsepower is way the heck more impressive when lassoed spread-eagle to the nose cone as when hunkered down in the blockhouse.

The reason our father suggested a heifer for its rodeo potential is because he figured the only way he was gonna survive to old age with a degree of comfort was to get us to do the uncomfortable portion of the farm chores. As required he had to find a means to dummie us up lest we run off to the Marine Corps for relaxation. Hence the heifer-rodeo comment.

We fooled our old man. We weren't taking no chances saddlin' a heifer next to the fence, where the suddenness of it all might upset her refined senses. We were some smarter than that. We'd do it indoors. In the barn. In the calving stall. Where the transition could take place slowly, gradually, incrimentally. As is required for females, same as if our maiden aunt had seen "Last Tango in Paris" a couple times before stumbling into that magazine store. Done well and sequentially, that heifer could do no else than act in a civilized way. Nobody gave a thought she might try and fit through the barn window with a kid attached. And while the clearance was pretty good on the bottomside, the top clearance left something to be desired. Which, as it happened, is where the kid was.

We ain't saying which of the brothers was scraped

together afterwards with fluids leaking from his ears. The flow stopped about three months after, though his ears still ooze wax enough to polish a Buick.

The books say John Glenn took eight gees during his launch into space; they say an F-18 in extreme unction can to go eleven gees, though they might have to shovel out the pilot. A holstein heifer is capable of seven gees when milked the first time. Same animal will pull nine gees if saddled in the barnyard on a sunny day. Saddled indoors, with a twelve-light window in the way, same animal is good for three more gees.

It isn't that you feel your brain slap against the back of your skull, as much as you feel it try to exit your ears.

I've seen what they call rodeo a time or two on television.

That ain't rodeo.

Rodeo is a twelve-light barn window, and a first-time heifer with a surcingle and vacuum milker attached. The kid might yet be attached, if he cleared the window.

Hot Story

I went to the neighbor's yesterday, it was 90 in the shade. Least that is what the thermometer on the north side of the shed read. 90 degrees even. Humidity about the same.

"An insufferable heat wave," said the radio. "Dangerous. Life threatening. Everybody should spend at least a couple hours in an air conditioned room," a solemn voice intoned.

Admittedly, it was Public Radio that said the heat wave was insufferable, which is true only if the person saying this is ensconced in an air conditioned room, and doesn't have to leave.

I do not like air conditioning. This is because I am of an age that can remember when the only places as were air conditioned were the dark confines of taverns. Once, in ancient and primitive times, air conditioning was so exceptionally rare it was advertised. I remember those neon lights, shaped to the words "air-conditioned" mockingly placed in the windows of taverns.

Being of Methodist extraction taverns were forbidden. A sense of strangeness surrounded taverns in general, much less the ones advertising air conditioning. I didn't know what was meant by air-conditioned. A kind of disinfectant perhaps, same stuff perhaps that we fumigated the barn floors with on summer evenings. The fog so thick you could break off a piece and chew it.

The farmhouse was not air conditioned. Much later our widowed mother was given a gift of an air conditioner to put in the window, one of the 110 volt units that quietly hum. I suggested at the time we find one of those antique neon signs from a tavern and hang it in her window; she being Old Order Temperance, was not amused.

I realize air conditioning in the modern work environment is exactly what renders people civilized during the hog wallow of summer. The reason some people go shopping in the summer is to enjoy the air conditioning of the mall. Air conditioning is now vital to the national economy; still, I think we are wienies. And that word is too slack to describe what happens to the character of average persons who become addicted to air conditioning; it is something much worse than soft, almost effeminate, something is done to the hormones by air conditioning.

Were America not quite so air conditioned, I guarantee there would be fewer parking lots done in the death-camp style. There is no greater cause to the air conditioned-culture than a massive, wall-to-wall, semi-gloss black asphalt, bumper-to-bumper parking lot. This is one of the most theoretically abusive artifacts possible, one that renders what is already hot and humid ten times worse. Too many people think green space and urban trees are only decorative, they think this way because they are air conditioned. "How quaint," is the comment on photographs of former tree-shaded streets, streets with trees towering over. Trees that get in the way of billboards, trees occupying perfectly valuable space, trees obscuring the commercial landscape. How did our ancestors get any business done in such an unkempt environment?

Were America not air conditioned we could guarantee another response. That those who hate morning, who can see no relevance for waking up with first light and going to work in the early hour... would come to love morning cool. Imagine great masses of ordinary people who voluntarily, voluntarily mind you, go to work at 5 a.m., maybe even 4 a.m. At 4 a.m. in mid-summer when the light is low and serpentine. At 4 a.m. the cardinal has yet to claim the air waves. The modern citizen watches the full length of the late show and then an episode of "Cops." They feel their blood coagulate at the mere thought of 4 a.m... because they are air conditioned.

It once was otherwise, the world was, and I remember the world before air. I remember summer worship at Liberty Corners when the pianist added a measure to the introit because it took that extra measure to get the seat of the pants ripped loose from the pews in order to stand up for the hymn. As a kid I liked that sound, that special summer cord rising from the pew, as the congregation tried to lift off.

Sundays there were when the congregation gave up on that hot little kirk and went to kirk at Camp Cleghorn on the Chain of Lakes. Like as not our only chance to swim in a real lake instead of an irrigation pit. Wearing trunks was a weird sensation, almost ruined the experience, except there were females, some with exposed belly buttons.

As a kid, I found God was easier business at Camp Cleghorn. God is nearer to the sawdust than to varnished maple, nearer in the darkness of the barn-tabernacle and hymns you had to bellow in order to dent the dark of that place. The picnic under the trees was of bologna sandwiches and potato salad. God can be described by a bologna sandwich; nothing fancy; white bread and mayo, pickle, onion and cold bologna. No picnic table, no gas grill, everybody sitting on the ground, even the old people who had to be lifted up from three sides when it was time to go. I remember the coolness of that oak-kept ground. As a kid I learned there are things that diminish God to the point of irreverence; air conditioning is one of them.

Coming Clean

T he bath is one of those singular distinctions between villagers and the farmers, and beyond, one
that never fails to separate the weekend hobbyist
farmer from the high-gear, haybale-tatooed farmer. There
is no liability to this observation. Farmers are absolutely
more comfortable amid the veritable beatitudes of dirt
than any other human being including a few number
of natural animals. A villager might admire dirt and
stand the depth of it momentarily, but as soon as release
is available, a villager enters into a covenant with soap
and water.

I have friends who bathe seemingly constantly. They
get up in the morning, having done nothing to this point
beyond snap their eyelids open, and they shower. They
go to work, they sit at a desk, in a vacuumed office, moving white paper for a living, they go home, take off their
clothes, they bathe. A significant number of these also
bathe before going to bed. Saturdays they play four innings of baseball, never once do they slide into base or
get into a fist fight at home plate, they return home, they
bathe. Before going out later in the evening they repeat
the water and soap fixation. They jog, they bathe. They
rake leaves, they bathe. They make love, they bathe.

All this bathing is curious, more so when the people

doing it are not dirty. This is an American obsession, this compulsion to cleanliness, to wash until we fairly glisten. Another odd thing is, while doing this people use soap that smells like a combination bawdy house and funeral parlor. They carry this smell around with them for the rest of the day. It confuses bees, confounds hummingbirds and the average workplace smells like a dead flower shop. If lost in the wilds far from civilization, these people can never be found using blood-hounds. The dogs would end up in mausoleums, in funeral corteges or dig up the neighbor lady's flower bed. It is this far people have come from smelling like people.

I have to confess of being another sort, the rural form. It is not that rural people do not bathe, shower or use soap; we do but it hasn't resulted into a paralyzing psychosis. Rural people are not constantly cleaning, there are reasons for this.

Originally, rural types bathed on the basis of the availability of the central resource. This period, known to my older sister as "the Second Frontier," being the time period just after the cutting of the pinery and "the coming of the messiah to the rurals." This is her expression. It is more commonly called REA or the Rural Electrification Act. To most it meant incandescent light and the junking of the kerosene lantern. It meant vacuum milking machines, toasters, radios, central heat. To my sister REA meant indoor.

Any astute reader knows what I mean by indoor. Indoor wasn't toast, wasn't radio, wasn't vacuum milkers or fanning-mills. Indoor was toilet. What an uncle called "toil and let." Indoor was flush, it was tissue paper, it was a whole heck better than corn cobs and pages from the catalog at 42 below. In short, indoor was warm, and it was a lot less likely to collapse into the very pit than the average fate of the two-holer. By the time I was born, the dark period of "the Second Frontier" was over. The savage landscape had been tamed and all, or almost all, was indoor.

What the bath consisted of previous to REA I can only recount as the legends were told to me. Water, according to the myths of old, was heated on cast iron stoves and dumped raw into copper kettles, tin tubs, hog-boilers and other uninspiring containers. This was commonly done in the kitchen, usually on a Saturday night and it was only once a week if you were lucky. If you were real lucky you missed the chance entirely. This was when lavender soap counted for something, it covered the chicken-scalding stench of honestly dirty people attempting to extract themselves from the previous shell. This bathing was in the great Roman tradition, it was a semi-public event. An event Alfred Hitchcock would have had a pretty hard time turning into the spine-softening article that he did to the shower stall.

I am nevertheless a child of the Second Frontier. The bath is still pretty much Saturday night. This doesn't include swimming, a hose down behind the shed, a dalliance in the stock-tank or hanging your feet in the creek. I came from people whose view on the bath is if your legs ain't glued together you don't need a bath and if you do, you're Baptist. Hose off your crotch, change the step-ins to a lighter color but don't waste water and leave clean till Saturday night.

According to my people the bath was like church, exactly like church, it was once per week. Any more marked you as an extracurricular sinner, it was a demonstration you weren't comfortable with life. It, bathing, like going to church, was a sign you were feeling more dirt than you probably had the right to feel or else had been up to something more dirtful than ordinary and that problem is covered by the Commandments, which is another scrub brush entirely.

It sorta bothers me when I go to a farm meeting if in

the atmosphere of hand soap and aftershave I cannot detect the more clinical smell of farmer. It worries me some when I think farmers might be going the same squeaky-clean way as villagers. Besides, I like the smell of 10W40 and gear oil has a particularly pleasant scent. Then there is silage and new potatoes and sand farmers and loam farmers and even sweat. The reader might think it odd but I like the smell, the hot tin-roof smell of sweat. I mean good copious sweat not your stopped-up niggardly villager sweat. It is dabbit curious and maybe somewhat funny that the people who read the labels to see if food items have preservatives or added chemicals haven't smelled like human beings for years and maybe generations.

I have a woman friend in Minneapolis, a stranded farm girl. Sometimes when I want to tease her that a masters degree and a $50,000 per annum job ain't the whole wash-tub, I send her an envelope of corn silage. Or a handful of new spring dirt, or a purple applicator of Doctor Elias' Teet Dip. I know for a fact she puts the stuff under her pillow and goes to sleep dreaming ruralisms.

I remember a barn building once, I was just a sliver of a board foot myself. The day was woeful hot and the neighborhood men had been lifting boards and hammering some hours. The air was still as the nose hairs on a corpse and an impious sun shone down hard and uncaring. The smell of these men in their labors was thick as oat chafe in an August granary, any more would have smarted the eyes. It was the very same overwhelming smell I found years later at the North Sea off the coast of Scotland. The same durable, ancient, honest-made smell.

When my father died my brother took home the work clothes Pa had been wearing that day. His wife told me, for a couple weeks after he lifted them to his face to smell our father again. Like I said, there is the farmer kind and villager kind and no else in between.

Catapult

Whose fault it was in the first place is hard to say. My older brother had the habit of engendering ideas in the head of his younger brother that in the end got the younger banished to the outer territories. For the older brother the notion had been entirely theoretical and never intended for human consumption. Not that I recall him saying this, but that was his line of defense at the trial.

Was he, the elder, who first said "catapult"? As I recall, the very word was charming, exceptionally charming, downright intoxicating it was. Catapult... cat-a-pult... sounded like something real interesting to do with a cat.

As I've said once or twice before, the cat is the farmstead's liquid asset. If experiments are necessary, the cat is the patient of choice because we had without trying a surfeit. Cows died, calves died, chickens, pullets, piglets, sheepits, all manner of agricultural beasts died and for no good reason, died despite the very best veterinary efforts to alter their fate. Died in flocks, swarms, groups, litters and congregations. Nothing with money invested in them died one at a time. They went like tourists, cheap-seat conventions of them flying to the hereafter at a discount.

Cats on the other hand were reluctant customers to the hereafter. They could hardly be compelled to go, whether the ticket was free or not. The farm had as a result a surplus, which wouldna been so bad if they were good for something. If only the French had ordained a delicate fare using cat as the raw ancestor. Never mind every other animal on earth had been made to suffer the rigors of cuisine, even some animals anybody in their right mind knows are inedible. Like squid, snails and lobster. Like pickerel. Like fish eggs. The French are capable of torturing every living thing, they have but to perfect the sauce and the world soon after is happy for the company at supper. This of an animal as won't make a good purse.

Farmcats are unkillable. It isn't that cats had nine lives, or nineteen, or ninety. They would not relinquish a single one, never mind all nine.

The word, catapult, came to me as a kind of revelation. When the older brother mentioned catapults had been used to beseige castles way way back in the time of King Canute and Rufus the Ugly, I knew why cats had been put on earth. Immediately I set up a research laboratory whose goal was the longest hang-time catapult in the history of seige weapons. For this I assayed the entire school library, finding not a single pertinent volume on seige weapons, much less an engineer's blueprint. So much for libraries being any use to a kid. Some while after I discovered in a Sunday School pamphlet, believe it or not, some heathen horde being pounded to dust by prehensile Christians using, what else, a catapult. The drawing was intended for background so it did not reveal a surplus of engineering detail but I could see a catpult was essentially a guided missile launcher utilizing some kind of spring device. The one in the picture appeared to use ropes.

Basically a catapult makes intentional use of whiplash. A teeter totter with a little kid on one end and a big fat one on the other is a catapult. A corresponding and like principle I discovered while skidding logs through the swamp. How when the ground freezes and you run over a black ash sapling with the tractor, bending it over so the log, following close on the heels of the tractor, is thrown a considerable distance by the same sapling. This is disagreeable if aimed toward the tractor.

As luck had it, I found in my home county the very best sort of catapults. Ditching had years previous excavated the meandering streams of the marsh leaving spoil behind in great somnolent humps. On these dry banks grew the hardiest tree this side of Baffinland, whose roots sought out subterranian moisture twenty leagues beneath, as a result the most securely anchored trees on earth.

Cats are what catapults were made for else they wouldna been called catapults in the first place. I can't be blamed for the subsequent treatment of the animal if the word and a bunch of derivations started it in the first place.

Getting a cat in a catapult is not easy. The burlap sack worked well, providing ventilation and room to exercise, at the same time containing the cat. An interesting phenomenon is the sound effect of a cat in a gunny sack, sounds exactly the like of a sonar-driven torpedo headed toward a doomed freighter, neow-neow-neow.

Cocking the catapult required my father's fencing winch. Once the sapling was bent to the ground, all I had to do to launch the cat was cut the twine, same as pulling the lanyard of a breech loading cannon. The limbs of the sapling were trimmed leaving a flat surface of branches on which I placed the sack. It was during this very time the Soviets had launched a dog into space without hope of retrieval and nobody thought it cruel.

Surely my launching a cat who would return to earth was a good deal more humane. Besides, everybody knows you can't kill a cat.

I discovered for the benefit of science that in-flight cats yield an even more remarkable noise. A long heart-rending Eoowwwww...that seems to hang and sting the air long after the cat lands. A sound, for earnest intensity, very comparable to a sonic boom.

A kid cannot watch a demonstration of this obvious exhaltation and not wonder what it feels like. I, after all, did not weigh much more than the cat and won't require no gunny sack.

From personal experience, the cool thing about a catapult is the resulting dizzy. Zero to sixty in a quarter second is fast, it plasters the stomach and the sauerkraut up against the spine so hard you can taste your backside. The problem, as might be guessed, is the landing. Luckily the creeks of the Buena Vista moor have bottoms so muddy you could land an asteroid there and they'd not spill a ripple. If manned flight is attempted, do it in a place with well-practiced mire, this I'm, sure why Cape Canaveral is a swamp.

Farmcats still thrive in the townships though some will not go near a black ash. Which is pretty much what I remember of it, the instantaneous whomp of that wicked tree, the landing about the same. As a kid I treasured the basic whollop, thinking myself indestructable if still in second place behind the cat.

The Great Camp

The image arrived in an exact rendition. We knew
instinctively every detail, every action without
reference to the *Boy Scout Handbook* or Ernest
Thompson Seton's *Two Little Savages.*

It came with June as part of the earth and air and every orphan feather and continued through July and not until the lists of August did it end. From the moment the school bell rang ending one year till it rang again at call of another, we were lost to the white and freckled races. On the impulse of summer and the uncivilized prospect of the farm we left all what was routine society and went to dwell in the manner of injuns.

History we knew had been unruly with our best chance. By the merest dislocation of a hundred years, at the most two hundred, we had missed the chance of being Indians ourselves. A measly hundred years and we might have existed in the sublimest installation of wild humans. How well we knew this awful failure, of time, of too many clocks wound overnight when at the slightest distance from us lay the chance of Mandan and Sioux, Crow, Arapaho, Nez Perce, Cheyenne, Blackfoot, Pawnee. We knew the names of all the buffalo and pony Indians. Knew every dog kettle and scalp rack in the tipi camps sprawled at the edge of creek willows. So narrowly we missed them, but for the pity of a hundred years we might have lived the greatest lives on the planet. We might have sang in the dust the hunt songs and danced into hollow earth the decoy call to a hundred million buffalo. We in a grass universe, carried on nothing more than a dappled pony, a loin cloth and obsidian spear.

Our intention was to correct the failure of historical time. To refurbish and install on the power of our imagination the zenith of prairie peoples and so equalize for the moment our ill-begotten fate.

Every summer we became "Injuns." The first act of which was to cut our hair in a griz so short the white curls of our brains showed through. This being the optimum choice because Ma wouldn't allow us the more glorious dimension of braids or the mohawk. The final transport to "Injunism" was the establishment of the great encampment behind the ice house, screened from the farmstead by a swath of lilacs and boxelder. This was the territories. On one side the white way of meat loaf, bathtubs and Sunday School, on the other the "Injun" prairie extending from the lilacs as far back as Gilman's woods.

The most important component in all this acquisition, what made the "Injun" camp real and inviolate, was the tipi. No swarthy wigwam of the woodlands, instead the temple of tents. The Crow lodge standing twenty-one feet from pole end to smoke wing. The major problem being the adjournment of the buffalo. How could we have a genuine tipi without buffalo hides? Here was the secret of "Injunness." When Ma forbid the mohawk we substituted the griz as a viable substitute. For the buffalo tipi we found a convenient replacement in the thousands of fertilizer bags used by the farm. Deftly stitched together they created an earnest wrap, equal to twenty-one foot popple poles. Our lodge was the equal of any in the classical age done of the finest heavy gauge fertilizer bags.

The lodge was impressive, it dominated the lilacs. Those popple poles gave it a cubic capacity far beyond our needs and became in due course the den to hang our war prizes, our totems, the place to dry Keds. A proper tipi has warrior space. Catlin's paintings showed exactly how. Volume was a necessary function of the prairie people, no crouch of the puptent, no hunkering of the wigwam, I mean a tipi is imperial, Noah's Ark was only a little bigger, even if ours was made of fertilizer bags and smelled some of fertilizer. The best ammonium sulfate fertilizer, heavy gauge polymer bags.

We could've found room for ten of us but there was only three, me and Gary and Tommy and then only when Tommy Soik's ma let him. Real Indians eat their dogs. We thought about that some, maybe Indians knew something about meat loaf we didn't. Thought about eating puppies but didn't know how to cook 'em. Besides, it kinda spoils your vision of Indians when you think of them eating dogs.

The tipi was better than a bedroom, held more stuff 'cause it had more corners, whole thing was corner and besides we built a fire in the middle which don't ordinarily situate itself in a bedroom. For weaponry we had B-B guns, jackknives, matches, spears with obsidian points if not quite obsidian. Uncle Scrooge comic books, a box of science fiction, Ma made us take pajamas but we never used them. No point in even trying at "Injun" with pajamas on. I figured we were the most complete remnant of injuns anywhere in the world those half dozen summers between 1952 and the Russian Sputnik.

The chores remained and instead of demeaning our station, those hours spent on hay balers and mowers were assimilated and became recomposed in a fit of "Injun" days. The alfalfa field and the marsh hay became the looming distance of the prairie. If we didn't have a spotted pony we did have a Ford model N and an Allis Chalmers model WD. Scalps were the real lack. We didn't have scalps and you can't very well be "Injuns," even revisionist "Injuns" without scalps and that bothered us something awful. 'Course it shouldn't have 'cause right there in the witness of every farm was the exact remedy for scalps.

Cats, we had cats and cats were always hunting the gophers along the road and in consequence getting killed. Marvelously killed and stupendously flattened into a two-dimensional representation of a three-dimensional cat. We had our scalp. Hung on a lodge pole it worked exactly like scalps are supposed to, it kept off foreigners. It marked the space behind the ice house and lilacs as "Injun" territory and Ma never even once came in to see if we were wearing pajamas. Snakes worked good, too, snakes and flattened toads and cow skulls. Ma never asked the whereabouts of bath and soap the whole summer as long as we kept to the lodge. A bath ruined our complexion, except the time we rubbed ourselves all over with the juice of butternuts and came out so brown we looked more "Injun" than the Indians.

Beneath the boxelders, behind the ice house, somewhere west of the Missouri we cooked supper on cow pie fires. Hubcap stews stirred with a stick. In the dark we raided the nearest settlers house for a still warm loaf of bread, a pan of cookies, the entirety of one platter of chocolate cake. This being the "Injun" way. Raids for new potatoes and sweet corn, slithering in loin cloths, our white ancestry camouflaged with char face. The hen house knew our stealth, the shadows we were as we tore white eggs from their beds and ate them fried and begging for mercy at breakfast.

Nights we in the least measure of loincloth terrorized

the neighbor's dog, stalked apples and stole the neighbor lady's brassiere. This was the prairie moment, we
ran among the cows who could detect on us no smell of
anything humanoid. We watched white people in their
houses, they were curious things, our fingers itched for
our scalp knives. We left stovewood on the doorstep of
the outhouse as a sign.

   With September, morning frost and school, we took
down the lodge, scattered the fire stones and went back
across the Mississippi, encountered the dread soap and
water baptism and became white boys again.

The Gate Keeper

Once in that former principality and kingdom of cow, in the land of gambrel and Moline, once there were gates, gates everywhere because cows were everywhere. For the kid raised on a dairy farm, the first commandment, the one before honoring God was "close the gate." Honor, sanctity, adultery, lies, robbery and murder mattered, but only after the gates were closed.

As with all lessons moral and behavioral, the lesson of the gates took a while to learn, took certain commission of omission to gain the habit that appeared to the casual observer entirely automatic. Whether or not a cow was in sight. It never ceased to amaze those subjected to this legal procedure the attractive force an open gate exacted on an otherwise empty and cow-less pasture. To the reasonable child there appeared no first rationale why the gate should be closed, not a cow in sight. Never mind it was such a bother. Meant getting off the tractor, unlatching the gate, getting on the tractor, driving the tractor and implement through, getting off the tractor, closing the gate, getting on the tractor. And not a cow in sight. So what was the deal about leaving that gate lay there until whatever you were doing is done? As said, not a cow in sight.

Perhaps because my personal learning curve is so much more the parabola than the straight line, I learned the hard way to keep the commandment, the first law of gates. Purgatory was not routinely or theologically a Methodist appliance but in the kingdom of cow, chasing cows is a close and real substitute. In the elementary school I went to, an identifying strand united those kids tutored by gates, who had been perfunctorily educated by gates both done and undone; the difference was straight-forward. These were children with legs and lungs gained not from jogging or basketball but from chasing cows, also spring heifers and the occasional horse. Running down a horse a time or two is sufficient apprenticeship to gain compliance to commandment number one.

It is known among ruralists that once a cow passes through an untended gate, all its faculties come to acute attention regarding the location of the gate, and it will thereafter avoid at all costs surrendering to that portal. As a result every good field required two gates, one to admit normal passage, the other to recollect the mischie-vous bovines who simply will not re-pass the scene of their original trespass. Science has yet to discover why this might be; never mind, it is so, explaining the second gateway to every field. It is still hard for me to believe that for all those years we were playing mind games with cows... mind-games with an animal whose cerebellum is the size of a washtub but whose cerebral knot is more akin to an acorn. How it happened we were playing mind games with such a creature is hard to explain unless you have pursued the damn beast halfway across the town-ship, coughing up your lungs at several junctures in this contest of wills.

The gate commandment in my township was rigidly observed. Didn't matter whether a farmer was more or less prosperous, whether they were Catholic or Wet

Baptist, the gate command was kept. While there were numerous and frightful examples of farmhouses needing paint, of barns and granaries in want of boards and window putty, rare was the example of a poorly done fence. Lying to the IRS, speeding, drinking and driving, skipping church, failing algebra, allowing ball joints to go ungreased was one kind of sin, stealing apples and asparagus was still another. However, there was no redemption for the sorry useless enemy of God who left the gate open. We knew well there was a level of hell for murderers, a lower one yet for Adolf Hitler and Joseph Stalin, and a lower, still more excruciating torment for those who failed to mind the gate. Explaining why the farmstead itself might go a wee bit dilapidated because a wise and reverential mannie spent his spare energy proofing the gate.

As explains Cousin Harry. If Harry did one perfect thing in his life it was his banjo-wired gate. As the fates conspired, our farm had forty acres located beyond the road eighty of Cousin Harry. This meant we had to cross his field to get to ours... and pass through his gate. His banjo-tuned fixture strung up tighter than the only Lutheran at a free-liquor bar mitzvah. It took a full ten minutes to engage sufficient muscle energy to open Cousin Harry's gate, and ten minutes more to reclose the same. To make matters even more interesting, Cousin Harry had divided his eighty into neat ten-acre fields, each with a line fence and gate. All of them banjos.

There were years we didn't mow the hay on that back forty because we couldn't summon the strength to go through all those gates. Happily, it was a low field and given to blue stem and Canada lilies so it didn't matter much whether the hay came off or not. Eventually we learned the trick to the closing of Cousin Harry's gates. The farm fashion was to string more wire high on the fence rather than low so the leg of the gate pole was longer on the bottom than the top. The solution then was to put the bale over the top of the post, then while on your hands and knees, like as not with your arms wrapped around the home post, heave the gate pole into its stirrup. Took five minutes. We thought this the easy solution.

When I was in high school I pinned my best friend Richard in wrestling class in eight seconds flat. He asked how that was possible being we were the same scrawny size, though Richard was Junction City scrawny. One weekend when he visited the farm I had him close one of Cousin Harry's gates.

"Jesus ..." is what Richard said.

My mama didn't like it when we said the Jesus when we meant another word. Mama didn't close the gate.

The Stick

I t is that I collect them. Sticks. Out in the corner of the garage I have cut the top off a 30-gallon oil barrel to store my collection. Sticks.

I started with sticks when I was a kid on the farm. It was my duty to steer animals many times larger than my own self, and who for personal reasons were adverse to the chosen path. At the time I was of small measure even for a farmkid and a stick made up the difference. Everybody knows you can herd cows better with a stick than without, especially if the bulk volume of your person isn't implicitly authoritative. Being a kid, mine wasn't.

Soon enough I understood the range of accomplishment and prowess a stick provided. I didn't have to yell at the cows with a length of elm in hand. My voice wasn't exactly commanding, especially if I wanted it to carry any distance. I discovered another thing, a stick is like having a third leg. I could take obstacles like puddles and cow pies using the stick as a spring board. Same with a barb fence I wouldn't ordinarily try. Using the stick I could take it. The stick gave me leverage on the world. If there was something suspicious down a burrow, I'd send the stick in after it instead of my hand. I could poke around dead things. And stir slime. The stick got a cow's attention a lot faster than "hey you." I'd climb a tree and prop the stick crossways in the branch, and sit there comfortable as a bluejay. And I could reach an apple that wasn't otherwise available to a zoological this side of a giraffe, unless it had a stick.

After awhile the stick became part of my body, sure enough it added to my backbone. Before the stick I always had to get my brother to go camping because I was afraid to go tenting by my own. With the stick I didn't need my stupid brother who'd sleep anyway, sleep during the worstest part of the night when monsters are the thickest. Myself, I always have been sort of wakeful and the stick helped. I'd sleep a while, then keep watch while the stick slept. A real good stick had eyes. I learned this when poking into badger holes and peering into squirrel dens. Don't know exactly how it worked but I could see in a squirrel den as if there was an eyeball attached to the stick. Darnedest thing it was.

Once a person gets the habit, sticks become a natural companion and a collection ensues. Less a collection than a circle of friends. Besides, sticks get old. Elm dries out and it ain't got the ol' tally-ho in it any more and deserves retirement. I couldn't bring myself to burn the sticks, and that's why a barrel of them is in the garage. Like the matched set from the summer my wife-to-be and I worked as camp counselors, those kids got a better education than what they paid for. Some sticks are plain, others have notches in them for God knows what reason. There's a stick used many years in the tater shed. Instead of poking my finger at a motor or conveyor as ought be moving, I'd poke my stick at it. That I yet have all my branches and twigs is due to the stick getting bit off, not my own self. Which leads me to think every farmer and mechanic ought have a stick. To venture where flesh must not with the power on, and we all know you can't tell what's wrong when the power is off, hence the stick.

After a couple seasons the stick resembles a war veteran and deserves a pension. By which time I've got my feel so integrated with that stick I can look around corners and underneath. My wife makes me put it away when the neighbor lady stops by wearing her mini skirt.

Being older, I like a stick I can talk to. Black ash has the highest intellect, but my preference is musclewood. Since talking to a stick isn't in the normal range, I carve a face on the head. A primitive countenance, the kind seen in the glens of druids who thought talking to trees was sane enough if it had a face gnawed to. Never mind you can see all the faces you want in tree bark without resort to whittle, but the world thinks talking to a plain tree is clinical.

A stick is a good reference. If you can convince a stick maybe you've got a case and might risk it on the neighbor. If the stick doesn't think well of it, best keep the opinion home.

The Gaelic for a companionable stick is *maide caraid,* means friend stick, the label predates psychology. When folks wanted to talk to God or some other responsible, they did it through sticks and stones and assorted rubbish, none of which charged $65 an hour or sent the collection plate by.

Like a dog, a stick requires regular exercise. Let dust collect on a stick and it stops listening. Any walk will do; woods, city streets, parks, hills, cow lanes, hospital corridors. A stick isn't afraid of the dark and can cross an icy sidewalk with the confidence of a centipede. Lean on it, sit on it, talk to it, make music with it. Don't matter, it's willing. The woodlot is best, sniffing and poking and peering into things, a stick has the inquisitiveness of a beagle and the courage of a lioness.

Some are not convinced a stick is useful. Which is OK owing there ain't that much musclewood anyway.

Still, going at the world without a stick is dangerous. Remember Moses crossing the desert? What's he got in his hand? Or how about King Solomon all furry and wise, next to him on the couch is his stick. Every king and queen and belost wanderer had their stick, from Methuselah to Muir, to St. Thomas and Thoreau. Makes me think the Oval Office be wise to import a case of musclewood from Wisconsin and pass them out at the next Cabinet meeting.

The Pit

The smell was like every summer day. The air had layers, each with its own density and origin, each with its own smell. The atmosphere was a laminate of farm country at hay time. Smells wandered, were caught in eddies and were held unaccountably long, then to collapse and yield to others. The smells were lined up, one behind the other. Each distinct, found in a separate layer on a still hot day.

The layers of summer smells no farm child forgets, there exists an entire atmosphere of hay. A kid after a while comes to have a nose for hay and can sort out the layers. There is a layer belonging to new mown, one for clover, another to alfalfa, still another of marsh hay and joe-pye weed, a layer too for the hay at the roadside cut by the town mower including a swipe at crabapple and rabbit nests. A smell at noon when the sun is full and hot and bearing down on morning cut hay, a smell when it has rained, and the night was heavy. Hay is a smell when it is right and every farmer knows just by smelling the hayfield though half mile away.

A farmkid's life is obsessed by smells, he knows through his olfactory lobes when it is time. Whether hay time, silo time or potato time, he can smell what is about to happen, smell those certain sweats, the hot grease in the pitman, the stale breath of haymows. With a little practice a kid learns to smell the farm and all the farms around as they bend to the task of hay. And every other for that matter.

If he is wise he learns to smell everything, rain and drought and the night before early frost. The smell of October when the ground is ripe with taters, when the chicken coop has a too-thick layer of gunpowder nitrates. To learn as is the way of farmers the smell of new tractors and painful stink of new debt and to know well the difference.

Inside the skull of every being as ever was a farmkid is an else smell. I remember it as a lurid smell, what I then thought was lurid. Like a boudoir was supposed to smell. It came, that smell, separate from all the other airs and layers of farm country. The gosh darn day spent lathering up the result of hay bales, in the most torturous kind of sunshine as turned a kid's body somewhere between brown, black and hay chafe. Among those layers of smells the thinnest, sorriest, most beckoning layer of all, a smell as only came in snatches like SOS code from a sinking ship. Dots and dashes that blinked inside my skull.

Others smell the same thing but it had no reference for them. Some, if they do smell it, think whatever it is smells... sorta off, smells darn unpleasant, more like putrefaction than anything nice. Like I said before, a boudoir. The difference is they have not inhaled that smell between layers of hay fields when the farm is a veritable gulag of new mown. Folks who lived in an atmosphere without hay cannot have a favorable response to that layered thin smell of putrefied boudoir water.

Once every forty, every woodlot had a pit, an irrigation pit dug in amongst the vast treasure of sand to find the secret under-pool. A pit with ten feet of the most boy-killing cold water as found anywhere on the earth,

water worth nothing for swimming because it'd kill ya
to try. Water to draw your hazelnut level with to your
adam's apple, the residue being a soprano fit for the
Metropolitan.

Farmkids didn't learn to swim in irrigation pits. Farmers were too much in a hurry for water to dig gradual
and allow a bathing beach as might give a kid a chance.
The irrigation pits had no gradients, they went from 0 to
12 feet in as cruel a slope as sand will stand. Learning
to swim in a pit wasn't possible. You didn't learn, you
either swam or died, no middle ground. Either you were
a fast-study or you weren't. A kid had to know this about
himself before he tried.

Smelling that layer of stagnant pit water, of dying
tadpoles and algae, sandwiched between hay smells
convinced most kids they were gonna swim. Heck, they
already knew how. The pit lured the kid. Sometimes
whole bunches of kids. The moment it happened always
the same, a couple hours yet till sundown and the air
temperature still 140 degrees, just finished with the last
load into the mow and all gummed together with hay
chafe and cow sweat and roasted freckles. One smell
of pit air and you didn't care whether you knew how to
swim or not, you were gonna try or die. Besides, maybe
it was true if you jumped off the bank and landed exactly
in the center of the algae you wouldn't break through.
Who ever said so was mistaken and knew it.

Soon as you jumped you knew, too, knew it weren't
true. Soon as your toe hit the algae the whole damn
sheet of it pulled back and smacked you into water a lot
colder than 140-degree day made right. Plunging like a
uranium bullet toward the bottom and the algae closing
the lid tight after. You know you're dead.

Boy, are you ever dead. You don't even know the first
thing about swimming and here you are trying to do it

in absolute darkness with no indication of what side is up and dab blasted cold besides.

Lots of farmkids died in the pits without even trying to swim because it was, after all, better than haying. At least dead was cool. The rest learned to swim right there and somehow broke the surface of the green slime and took a lungful of air tasting better than you thought regular air could just a few seconds before. Swimming natural the same as it comes to frogs and turtles and water striders. They, the newborn of the pit, paddled around the pit till the sun went down and the country started to snap and crackle as it cooled off, same as a stove with the fire gone out.

I know of kids who walked home on those nights in the naked condition. Looking like oyster pearls in the darkness and better, feeling like pearls.

There were kids who lay naked on the lawns in the dark yards of farmhouses and smiled like they never knew was possible. They weren't even beatniks, but man were they cool.

Bringing Up
the Heifers

A thletes have a tendency to admire themselves, explaining why mirrors are important to their conditioning. Who can blame them? They are beautiful specimens if it's specimen you're after.

Farmers have a hard time with athletics because for all the hurry it has no end product; the spectacle is the thing. The result can't be baked, toasted, fried in olive oil, served on Polish rye or keep the cold out. Agriculture would like nothing better than to have a long list of chores — hay making, potato picking, stone picking, cucumber picking, morning milking and a few others — transformed into a national pastime the same as baseball. Then the term farm team would have meaning and athletes could feel useful because they'd have a crop to show for it. Add a dose of nubile, latex cheerleaders to morning milking and it wouldn't be the same dreary chore, besides having something decent to blame for why there is so much surplus.

The toughest sporting contest on the farm was bringing up the heifers. All summer long these beauties luxuriated on the back forty thinking they were Bohemian bovines without any civic responsibility. An athletic event is the consequence of reprograming the summer heifer's luxuriating mind. Bringing up the heifers in our township occurred in that part of November between fall plowing and liming the fields. It was deemed prudent to extract the heifers from the woods before deer season when, as routinely happened, a heifer was mistaken for a deer.

The local farmers helped each other because it took the numerical equivalent of a regiment to reeducate those heifers; farmers, mamas, pickups, grandmothers, cousins, girls, the lame, hired men, village drunks... we weren't very particular about who was on the team when it came to moving unpulpited heifers to their waiting catechism with the milking parlor.

If the way to the barn was on the town road, more folk were required to steer the heifers than if a fenced lane was provided. Still, a fence to a heifer is about the same obstacle as the Ten Commandments is to a Christian, and nothing a good running start can't overcome. The usual ploy was for participants to engage fright to keep the heifers from thinking rationally about how vulnerable the fence was. Every member of the round-up got a gunnysack and when a heifer started for the fence, a gunnysack got flopped in their direction. Heifers thought the gunnysack was something more than a gunnysack. An appendage human beings had heretofore concealed. A body part that was now lunging at them. Whether for purpose of consumption, procreation or predation the heifer had no idea. Mostly it worked.

One always escaped. Last seen headed to the Eden it had known all summer, taking the fence as gracefully as a steeple-chase colt and digging for the woods across the new plowing. It was here bringing up heifers separated itself from a mild-mannered sport to the deadly duel over who was going to kill whom.

New plowing is a lethal weapon. Tourists don't know

this. You cannot walk across it without breathing hard, running across it is homicidal. Soft is not a sufficient description, adding very to soft is still not equal to new plowing. Square and cube the adverb and it is still unrepresentative. A foot however cautious placed on new plowing sinks in four inches. A runner at speed sinks in eight. A farmkid wearing normal autumnal dress — high top boots, stocking cap, mittens, wool socks — might as well try running on water as attempt new plowing. The immediate resolution is to take as few steps as possible, the result less running than broad-jumping, the heifer by this time is doing the same thing.

Any cardiologist can testify running in new plowing is the most intense metabolic experience a person can have before they die. Heifers know this, too. They are born with the knowledge, which is why they wait their escape till the field adjoining is new plowing.

A 4 X 4 pickup with a ram jet for an engine cannot cross new plowing intact, and the smoldering remains tain't worth scrap. Neither can John Deere's best diesel match the pace of a freedom-loving heifer. The only missile capable of winning her back to the barn was the farmboy.

When bringing up the heifers, a couple kids were kept in reserve, same as pro football stashes away a Heisman trophy quarterback on the sideline. The boys were wrapped in blankets in the heated cab of the pickup, waiting for that moment when a heifer takes the fence and breaks across the field. The kid, wearing nothing but Keds and gym shorts is deployed after the wild hiefer like a heat-seeking missile. The whole business was merciless, knowing one contestant or the other will have to die. The kid at first gains as his pulmonary function soars but the heifer holds to its brutal pace. Then the kid's lungs start to liquify followed by the rest of his internal organs, the bones dissolve and from the distance we see him begin to smoke behind the ears. Finally his brain implodes, he stumbles and falls in a steaming heap. The heifer, now down to a wobble, staggers to the fence, stares in reverie at the woods just beyond, collapses and dies. Its comrades who've been watching the drama turn resignedly for the barn. The kid lying prostrate in the field is eventually retrieved, wrapped in a horse blanket and driven home for intravenous soup, having served up his life to the higher cause, which is the barn.

The heifer left for dead next to the fence struggles to her feet, the woods are no longer an option. Whatever was in that heifer as wanted the woods was killed off and in the low and cold autumn dark she turns for the barn whose warm lights she now feels a half section away. Somehow the place is better for that. And likewise the fate of being ever after the milk-heavy cow and never again fleet as a deer.

At the feed mill's winter caucus, the race is recounted, described in freeze-frame segments. Old farmers remember a time when they were the chosen one, golden and lithe, as fast as greased buckshot. How new plowing 'most killed them and wondering yet why nature didn't design lungs after the wide-mouth Mason. All real athletes wonder the same question, some don't have milk barn consequences attached.

The Fence Bucket

As a potato farmer I do not have the same obligation to fix fence as my neighbors who are dairy farmers. Potatoes are surprisingly antic at times, green beans even more so, but not so much as to jump the fence. Colorado beetles and green peach aphids however do jump fences.

What caused me to think on fence-mending was seeing in the back corner of the old granary a fence bucket hanging from a bent nail. Once every farm as tended cows had a fence bucket and it was a routine chore to walk every fence line during the spring to check the condition and, as my father said, put sing in the wire. That's how my father referred to a fence tuned to proper concert pitch. A good fence was said to sing, this from the tonal quality of the wire when tapped with a pair of pliers.

The poet Robert Frost observed that good fences make good neighbors. He did not go on to say why, as is the penchant of poets. The comely phrase, that good fences make good neighbors, continues to be discussed in English classes as a preposterous inversion of morality. Christians and psychologists do not wish to believe in fences in general, or that a specific goodness is based on the maintenance of walls, borders or privies, neither on moats or jagged obstructions. The poet Mr. Frost can feel smug to have generated such a long-standing debate that his simple observation plainly said.

Robert Frost did not delve into the intricate aspects of fence-mending having already caused sufficient damage to the establishment argument. Frost probably did not notice how a good fence sings. But then he was probably observing a stone fence not one of barbed wire. While a stone wall is the more classic fence than a five strand on cedar, I think it not so good at minding cows.

If farmers were more operatic, fences might be tuned to variable frequencies so that when the wind blew hard in March it could set loose a doleful dirge, whose effect on cows and neighbor dogs would prove interesting. I would be tempted likewise to tune my fence, to foil trespass. For this a melancholy note taught to prevail with only a little east wind, and as a result scare the bejesus out of those uninvited. I might if I can find the time, orchestrate a fence that will once in place protect farmland from subdivisions and shopping maelstroms. A fence that curses and hexes any who dare to think concrete or a straighter road will improve things.

Fixing fence was a universal duty when it came to chores; if nothing else was readily available, there was always… fixing fence. Any rainy day sufficed, with slicker and galoshes we were sent to fix fence; with a broad brim hat it was rather nice. Which explains why every good fence bucket had holes in the bottom, to drain the rain water off. Though the odds are the reason it became a fence bucket in the first place was it wouldn't hold water. The bucket is filled with old staples; bent over, crooked, splayed, tangled, prevaricated fence staples. Before they could be used they had to be straightened, which lent fence-mending another singular kind of charm.

The manual to fence repair suggested there were two methods to the repair of the sagging line. The quality approach was to first remove all the staples holding the line to the posts, attach a fence stretcher and retune the wire. If the wire was new and had come to sag, this is the proper way. The procedure was entertaining and could use up a rainy day. In the bucket was mash and the masher. The mash and masher were the two names for hammers in the fence bucket. The claws of the mash hammer were inserted under the wire with the staple centered in the claws, smucked in turn with the masher driving the claws under the wire so when rocked the staple came out. At one cedar post every rod, there are 80 staples to treat likewise with the mash and masher. Now the wire is ready to be regigged. As said, this is the quality approach. It is however so much easier to fix fence by simply driving in an extra staple slightly around the corner from the original and in this way snug the wire. Besides, if the wire was old and rusted it won't come off in one piece anyway, much less take the strain of the stretcher. So it was better just to snug the wire but it was heavy on staples, requiring two, three, maybe more before the wire was back up to pitch.

The central theme of fixing any fence was to slow down the animate soul that is by nature a careless soul and not incumbent to stay in any one pasture. Which explains theologians as much as it does the keepers of cows. The fence is an appliance of domestication the same as a clothesline and kitchen sink. It is a nice thing to find the cows in the evening where the morning had put them. It is easier on the cows even if they don't know it. I was a kid when I realized a lot of the things that people do, that grownups do are really fences. They might not look like fences but they are fences and their purpose is not to keep the cow in so much as prevent wear and tear on places where the pasture isn't any good anyway, or will kill the cow because it will over-indulge. The fence is good for the cow though the cow doesn't know it. This notion scared me then and still does.

The spring day was spent fixing fence, in between were patchy episodes of drizzle and sleet. The gloves had wet through long ago; working bare-handed was better anyway because barbed wire ate up cotton gloves. As a chore, fixing fence is not for tourists. Rare even that poets come by any more. Hawks do though and sometimes the sun breaks out and the slicker gets hung on the post. Not long after you fetch it again.

A person who has done this chore both professionally and repeatedly ought to be able to draw some conclusions on the standard reliquary statement regarding mending fence. And why the poet thought so well of it. Most farmers would sarcastically offer the poet was just visiting and that is why he spoke so kindly. Farmers ordinarily do not admit to poetry because poetry is demeaning, always too quick is poetry to reduce a common chore to something passionate. Passion, of course, can be sold in the best case at retail prices, which means tourists. Poets, farmers secretly believe, are nothing more than preliminary tour guides. Let a poet sing while fixing fence and the next thing you know there's a paved road leading to it and a parking lot. Followed after by an engineer-type who wears a hard hat while fixing a tourist sample length of fence, he works eight hours with coffee breaks, he goes home if it rains. Much less sleet.

Was a poet who said a good fence makes good neighbors; the farmer doesn't want to see the neighbors much less their cows. Even less the tourist who thinks a fence might be photogenic.

My Sister
Invented BGH

My sister invented BGH. Not that we knew it at the time, but she did all the same. It was her. One day she was a skinny kid, worse, a skinny farmkid. Besides, she was a girl... with freckles... and legs so skinny a walking stick looked downright meaty by comparison. And the next thing we knew she went from fence-post ugly to premium predatory voluptuousness, spending sexual pheromones and encouraging wet dreams wherever she went without any sense of remorse. It was a miracle, what happened to our sister, to this farmgirl... equal to Moses opening the Red Sea... of Lazarus waking from the dead... of the loaves and fishes enough to feed the bowling team. She was just as skinny as before and freckles disfigured her nose but nobody noticed she was the same skinny farmkid.

That was 1952. I remember the year 'cause Dad had the ugliest car in the world. A splitting wedge had more style than that car. It was useful enough but irreconcilably ugly. Which is how cars were supposed to look in 1952. Folks in 1952 were still suffering the basic human gratitude for not having to walk. The modern car had not yet arrived. Air conditioning, power windows, heaters that worked, wipers that wiped, cars that started in the cold of winter without a quilt and a light bulb... they were still to come.　In 1952 Deluxe meant four wheels and a spare. Style had not yet arrived.

Our Chevrolet was not only ugly it was incurably gutless.　Never mind the installation of a genuine chrome-plated air cleaner from the J.C. Whitney catalog. Neither did a chrome tailpipe make any difference.　The only thing about to improve that car's velocity was a sheer precipice.　It was impossible to sit behind the wheel and imagine Juan Fangio or Alberto Ascari. Like I said, style had not arrived.

Being a farmkid I found BGH as no great suprise, a miracle maybe but no surprise. I had seen BGH in action a million times before.　Every heifer went through the same thing, went from a skinny no-account good-for-nothing heifer to dairy barn dreadnaught in the same rapid transition as my sister.　Before the effects of BGH took hold of her anatomy, a heifer can out-race a thoroughbred horse, leap a five-strand fence, out-corner a brown bat and generally disable every other creature in the book of Genesis.　After BGH, a heifer is no more maneuverable than a river barge, every animal instinct within it having been blunted save one.　The heifer became an eating, chewing biological factory whose sole purpose was to give ride to that milking machine twice a day.

1952 was a tough year on the farm, that when my sister invented BGH.　It was the same year black-and-white arrived.　Everything in agriculture was ruined in 1952, every standard overturned, every normalcy displaced. What had been a calm if not downright quaint red-barn farm out on the sand flats was after that in open revolt. Black-and-white was not only the arrival of television, which given the reception of the signal in central Wisconsin, was about as entertaining as watching oatmeal boil. Still, a lot of folks were watching oatmeal boil. It was the thing to do and could no more be avoided than breathing because it measured our style. A farmhouse without a television antenna was a heck farther out in the boondocks than a farmhouse with an antenna. Even my grandfather had a television antenna, he didn't have a television but he had an antenna.

Black-and-white meant the arrival of something besides television. It was this reception that bothered my old man. He didn't see television as much of a threat as was the other black-and-white invasion, genus Bos, a species original to the Holstein islands. Big, lumbering undulates as will out-milk a Guernsey two to one, even three to one and blame docile besides. The arrival of black-and-white on the farm were those of Bos Holstein. It marked the end of milk cans in a spring house, the end of wood-stave silos, and the end of the barn my grandfather had built from the pinery because it was no longer big enough. It was the end of the warhorses, of Percherons and Clydes, the end of the cheese factory at the crossroad. It was the end of innocence if there ever was any.

To our father, Holsteins were Nazi cows. They were something the SS and Gestapo invented in their biological laboratories. The Germans may have lost the Battle of Britain but they won the battle of the dairy barn with Das Bos. The genteel age of the Anglo-Saxon cow was over, gone were the country and mores of brown-cow agriculture. America hadn't been bombed by the Luftwaffe but it was in ruins just the same with Nazi cows the size of mastodons taking over.

Super Tits, Pa called them. Four-legged Jayne Mansfields cows. Guernseys and Brown Swiss are awful flat-chested after a farmer sees Holsteins in a tight sweater. Pa roiled, he damned and cursed, he swore blood oaths, and even threatened litigation. This, the end of agriculture as he knew it. Gone was the bright little farm, gone the community cheese plant, gone the classic milk can. From now on it was Grade A and bulk tanks as meant government inspectors and the dreaded whitewash three times a year. It meant an addition to the barn, more alfalfa, more land, more corn, more tractors.

In the end Pa surrendered and Adolf Hitler's gassoaked ashes grinned and uttered *sieg heil*. Their names were Sadie, Topsy, Lady, Sunflower and Rosebud. They were Deutschlander cows with hoofs the size of barrellids and milk as white as snow. Quarts and gallons of milk, pails and buckets of milk, foamy, frothy white milk, pure Arian milk. Milk less for cheese and butter as for gallons and jeroboams of milk to drink cold and fresh. No longer the kindly Guernsey yellow milk, yellow as a dandelion; after it sat a while in the refrigerator about as good to drink as a dandelion.

What I remembered was all that milk had to be carried the length of the barn. Not with pipelines, not in taxi cabs or elevator cars but by the nominal slave of agriculture, kids. It wasn't only milk, it was hay bales enough to fuel their violent bale sucking appetite. And cows the size of the Hindenburg can crap in like fashion, veritable foothills. Our lives soon became devoted to fulfilling every need of these Herman Goering bovines.

As a kid the way I saw it the U-boat nearly won WWI and the blitzkrieg and the Stukka nearly won WWII. Germans know why this is. They never intended to win the war, the German soul can not bear winning. Winning is anticlimactic, un-Wagnerian, the Loreli always must lure the hero and the nation to the rocks in the end. In the battle of Das Bos Deutschland had no intention of losing. They knew they could not, they knew the essential element of universal greed at the heart of man would respond to the siren song of white milk. They would sell their wives and children into abject slavery to keep Holsteins. We carried, we forked, we lifted, so did our sister. She was sixteen. She carried milk the length of the new barn, lifted the can over the edge of the strainer into the bulk tank an easy two feet over her head. We forked manure, silage, shoveled feed, bagged oats, threw hay bales, all to serve the Third Reich's Holsteins. So did she, our sister.

It was here precisely our sister went from a triple A to a solid B cup, obviously bovine growth hormone was at work. Where before she couldn't attract attention stark-naked in a tater patch, she now resembled a walking geographical facsimile. The Nazis knew this. If she kept it up, my sister would have had the sufficient chest to sing Wagnerian opera or at least serve in a beer hall.

Them Germans. That's how our father said it. Them Germans. A nasty conniving race, plotting at this very moment some new trick to redesign the world. The next thing you know they'll take a dumpy-looking car, turn it arse-backwards and try to sell this back-asswords business to the world. And the world caught up in the new style will swallow the bait. And the Germans will have won again even though they don't want to.

So maybe my sister didn't really invent BGH but it happened on her and changed her and everything else too. And if you ask me, Ferdinand Porsche sounds like a cow's name.

The Line

It stands east of the car garage, and is an unflinching metaphor. Everything else on the farmstead has changed. The barn was converted, the front porch enclosed, the chicken coop is gone entirely, grandfather's tractor is now a toy. But the clothesline is still there, where it has always been, next to a row of apple trees, just a little beyond the raspberry patch, the lilacs that flank the windward side were planted by Hiawatha.

The clothesline is symbolic of something more than some fine rural sentiment, how much more I can't rightly say. Something happens inside when I see a clothesline. How to portray the resulting emotion is not a scientific exercise. Whenever I see a clothesline I know some genuine under-paid, screwed-over humanity is close by. It is a similar sensation when a business-type person who ordinarily wears wingtips or black heels is seen going about in their stocking feet. I believe the casual evidence shows a lot of the consumer products surrounding us are there to aid our escape from the sense of commonness. Like those dark window treatments seen on cars and trucks, such is our desire to separate ourselves not only from the pedestrian mass, but from the view of the pedestrian mass. We pay a lot to be "hip" in America, so much do we pay that no small part of our overall industriousness is involved. The essential demarkation of all this is the label involved, and its price tag.

I realize that were we to subtract from our collective behavior all those products and ministrations whose purpose is to enthrone our egos, an awful lot of stuff would suddenly be missing from store shelves. I doubt there exists a single article or artifact anywhere in the world for which there is not a premium grade model. Many are the names on consumer items, with their slight variation on the theme, all those cryptic tags, those tasteful initials, those proofing marks, whether of cars, jeans, whisky, fountain pens, suits, teapots, wine, cigars ... what a reeking pile of superlative it all is.

I was once on the river Orinoco as flows through central Peru and joins a little ways beyond a consummate stream called the Amazon. The Orinoco is slow and muddy. Slower by half than the Mississippi and muddier by twice. The Orinoco has dolphins where the Mississippi only has catfish, though I think I'd rather eat a catfish.

The people who live and dwell along the Orinoco are very like the people who were living and dwelling on this river a thousand years previous. They live and die at the behest of the river, surnames here are hard to come by, no census is taken, few record their baptism. They live by hunting, fishing and gathering fruit. That they are so unchanged is because there is no overt reason to do so, the forest and river readily provide. Back from the river the old deities still reign, despite missionaries have tried. They do not shrink heads any more; there is less need, the severed head of a Barbie doll works just as well.

What struck me about these river people were their clotheslines. It was not so much the incongruity of clotheslines among people who, because of their tropical Eden had no obvious meterological loyalty to clothes, but because the clothesline seemed an homage to something basic.

If you go anywhere in the modern world, America or Europe doesn't matter, whether Japan, China, North Africa… there are places you will see clotheslines, and places you will not. I have never been to Beverly Hills though I have driven the length of North Shore Drive in Chicago and felt like quite the ethnologist, peering at some wonderous artifact of exceeding wealth. There were no clotheslines. Not one. If I asked, I would have been told it is ever so much easier to dry clothes in an automatic dryer. It probably is. Few would volunteer the answer that they wouldn't be caught dead with their washing exposed to public view.

As a kid in late pubescence, I did ride my bike past Mrs. Swantek's house every Monday evening during the summer. Mrs. Swantek was widowed by the Korean War but remained a while on the farm of her father-in-law. It was an isolated farm on a marsh road that went to Bancroft the back way, and since nobody went to Bancroft the front way, the back way wasn't heavy traveled.

Mrs. Swantek hung laundry for herself and three kids every Monday. I don't know why Monday was once the universal wash day, but it was. The clothesline ran from the back side of the house to a clump of boxelders. Like most clotheslines it was a tenacious thing. It had become ingrown to the boxelder on the one side, while the other end was rust-fixed to the back side of the house.

Every Monday Mrs. Swantek hung the wash, by which I rode my Schwinn bicycle. About sundown, two, three, four times I rode by, before leaving for home. Rode by Mrs. Swantek clothesline. Rode slow. As fat-tired Schwinn bikes were exactly designed for.

I grew up in that former age when seeing a brassiere was the same as seeing… flesh.

Mrs. Swantek moved not long after, probably in part

because of the strange kid who rode his bike up and down her road on Mondays during the summer. Where she went, what became of her, I do not know. I just want her to know she left behind one grateful kid, touched by her compassion for the sufferings of adolescence, and rural adolescence at that.

I distrust a landscape without clotheslines. A righteous land ought be flown over by bed sheets billowing and pillowcases inflated, by socks and shirts and undershorts. I say this because I have slept in bedclothes whipped by the wind... it has no need for scented fabric softener. I have worked in bib overalls sky-dried; they seem more lenient, more flexible to my task.

The clothesline is still on the house Mrs. Swantek left behind; the man who now lives there works at the potato plant west over about seven miles. They continue to use the clothesline, I see them and the kids hanging clothes on Saturday mornings. She teaches, so they wash on Saturday. A comforting sight are clothes drying, a simple and expedient chore. The clothes at first hang heavy and wet, slowly and furtively inhabited by ghosts a good land has, who humor and laugh among the clothes, then go to try another for size. It may be only the wind, yet I think it is something more.

Boom

The Fourth of July is a child celebration. Any average American cannot name the founding fathers much less retell of the amazing stew these planters, hot-heads and the occasional genius stirred against the generally enlightened authority of His Majesty.

At base and always, the Fourth celebrates the American spirit, the birth in the wilderness of a zeal for being what the world now well knows as the American character.

That we celebrate this holiday with noise is not solely an American trait but it is so like us. As a child this is why the Fourth of July so appealed to me, that it did rejoice in provocative vibration. Nothing it seemed to me then so countered the drear psychology of human gloom than a vivid loud noise, nothing stated the case for "I am" better than a classic cracker. If I was the biological child of bone and blood, I was also the construct of that classic formula; one part charcoal, one part salt peter, one part sulfur. If my blood ran red, my and every child's spirit ran the color of gunpowder, at least on the Fourth of July.

Why BOOM so mattered in my childhood I can not explain. My parents were good, I think they were Christians though you can never be too sure about Methodists. I suspect they went to the church for the sake of the convenience, so they didn't have to figure out things for themselves. As a kid I couldn't exactly tell what was convenient about this though I was led to believe the soul had something to do with it. Not that I ever saw one. The hymns characterized the thing as pretty darn plentiful but never addressed the business of exactly how big, whether it had a bone, a shell or was more gelatinous. My guess was a feathered sort of organ thought to roost in the precinct of the human condition. That it existed no where else immediately raised my suspicions. The substance of the plot as best I could determine was when a person died, the soul flew off, kinda like an ejection seat. Then it migrated, like geese and ducks migrate except the soul had never been that way before. Which again engaged my suspicions.

As a kid and especially on the Fourth of July I believed in BOOM, any noise in the general range of a thunder clap would suffice. I knew then of kids who were content to sniff glue and aviation gas. I was of the other desire, willing to stick my head inside a big bang. I had already discovered that the effect of a BOOM is dependent on the radius of its containment. Once I climbed inside a 50-gallon oil barrel and whopped a full roll of paper caps with a hammer. Golly that smarted. A really high quality BOOM is pretty much circumscribed by any remaining willingness to do the same thing over again. That I never again crawled in the 50-gallon oil barrel details how high a quality noise I had achieved, but I did tell my little brother how an ordinary roll of caps is increased to near nuclear proportions by an ordinary barrel. He went to prove it for himself and he didn't do that again either, demonstrating again the sterling quality of the BOOM in question.

I and my brother searched the world, at least our portion of it, for high quality noises. One of the best and cheapest was a green ash board about 12 inches wide and 12 feet long. One of us would stand on one end of the board laying flat against a plumb stretch of concrete. The other kid pried up the far end of the board, lifting it as high as he could, releasing it in unison with the other kid taking one step forward on the board, so it returned with distinct urgency to the concrete. The sound was easily comparable to a sonic boom and some bit better if the garage door was closed. Our mama did get a tad bit nervous any time we closed a door on the farm.

I think the highest quality noise we ever generated was when the town chairman substituted road culverts in place of the plank bridges on the sand roads crossing the marsh. Personally, I liked the low unruly rumble of a good plank bridge, not to mention the truly high quality rattle that comes from a gravel road when a driver realizes one of the timbers is out on the bridge and they either stop before getting to the bridge or they will stop slightly under the bridge. The speed limit on a timber bridge was about 15 mph and the culvert was installed in order to raise the speed limit. They did not ask my opinion.

The culvert, however, did add a new dynamic to our research into pedestrian explosions. Not only was the culvert a barrel-looking thing in the first place, but its close diameter acted the same on an otherwise small noise as the 50-gallon barrel. A roll of caps dispatched at once by a sledge hammer sent downstream a noise the size of a barn, that collided and ricocheted off the woods so what neighbors heard was a most ominous report. Four or five rolls of caps hammered off in rapid succession caused a sound exactly like the skirmish line at Little Round Top. We'd do this on the Fourth for Isaiah Altenburg, who was himself at Gettysburg. For a week after we heard people who were supposedly well-rooted to reality tell of sighting old Isaiah in his forage cap in the far woods when it was none other than five rolls of caps, a short-handled sledge and 50 foot length of road culvert.

Myself I thought it kinda neat to invoke the spirit of old Isaiah on the Fourth of July. To send a chill of cognition through otherwise resistant bones, to raise up in that hay-making township that grim moral tale of Union boys who never saw a slave in their life dying to set one free. I knew then the soul isn't something you have to weigh to know it exists.

The American soul has a fuse attached, sometimes it has been too noisy, too blatant, too impolite for our neighbors. But without this splenderous noise as is America, what a dull sane world this would be, whether that noise arose form T. Jefferson's pen, the township's culvert or Mister Elvis and his guitar, it is all the same, the sound of the American soul rattling the cage.

A Good Fine Smoke

After I discovered corn silk I knew the relentless stranglehold the tobacco companies had on the American populace. All that is necessary to get the item you want to sell into merchantile ministry is put it in the mouth of Raymond Burr or Frank Sinatra or Sargeant Joe Friday and millions of persons obediently follow suit. Stick a three foot length of lath down the pant leg of a movie star and within the week everybody who's the least cognizant of social order is hobbling after their example.

Corn silk had tobacco beat from the very beginning. Like I testified before, I tried most of the other stuff, wood chips, shavings, oat straw, bran meal, catalog paper, erasers, everything but auto tires and dead snakes I tried. They all failed on one or several accounts to satisfy the strict elements of smoking materials. A few burned too eagerly and I hardly had time for a breath of them before the fire went out. Some failed altogether to ignite. I looked forward to bran meal as a good smoke but it wouldn't light and a few smokes were just too blamed toxic to attempt.

A girl from Minnesota told me she smoked corn stalk, that being the section between the joints, she said it was a wonderful smoke. The girl at the outset was red haired and not to be trusted and had more lung capacity on her with several points of that capacity poking out the front of her shirt. The mechanical efficiency sure wasn't equal between us because I couldn't get corn stalk to draw. The far side lit alright but couldn't be persuaded to the other end. No matter how hard I sucked at it, I couldn't induce the smoke to follow. You might as well try to siphon a wishing well into a second floor bathtub, try that and the whole of you'll end up inside a length of garden hose the second you stop pulling. I didn't trust Minnesota girls after that.

What puts a kid off corn silk from the very beginning is corn silk is not what might be called short supply. Every ear of corn whether the cob is full kerneled or not has a scalp of corn silk attached and this the finest smoking material the world is ever likely to see. It lit good, it tasted excellent, it cost nothing.

I couldn't figure out after smoking corn silk why starlets and Perry Mason smoked tobacco when corn silk is so much better. I could roll a corn silk cigarette a foot and a half long using regular Buster Brown tablet paper and it drew like a Pall Mall. And a smooth smoke, you didn't have to suck your eyeballs into your nose to get the smoke from the far end to the near side. Granted, it did tend to fuse a bit and stray little sparks drizzled from it which weren't no problem and nice to watch besides. I thought it looked cool. I thought everybody'd think so.

My brother was four years older and a cynic on any subject I cared to mention being as I was the one who mentioned it. If Mahatma Ghandi said corn silk was a good smoke or Eddie Mathews, then it was a good smoke even though they were paid to say it. But if I said it because I knew it was a good smoke it was just "dumb younger brother." I could quote Wernher von Braun directly and to the millimeter but it didn't make any difference.

I knew the problem with corn silk, it was just too darn easy. For a thing to have any class it's got to be something other than easy. You can't have ten million acres of corn and expect people to smoke corn silk because it is too easy. Tobacco needs hoeing, the flowers snapped off and the leaves cut and hung and then auctioned off by the guy with a gallop for a tongue "...sold American," and then baled up to ferment with a secretive dose of company recipe. Then stamped into thin little cylinders neatly packaged in exactly, and I mean exactly, the right shape and size to fit a shirt pocket. It is my suspicion if they ever built the Bible to the same dimensions of a cigarette pack the whole world would Christianize in a couple weeks. A cigarette pack felt so good, so firm, I was invulnerable with a cigarette pack in the sleeve of my tee-shirt. First time I swiped a pack of cigarettes I didn't want to smoke it as much as feel it. It had a... a...intense feel to it, the same as how a pellet gun felt over a BB gun. I felt braver after touching a cigarette pack, kinda like I thought I'd feel after touching a brassiere. Like you know something a kid isn't supposed to know and that changes you. Same reason I liked to pick up .22 shells and just heft them, unfired .22 shells with the bullet still in them, there is some vital and tragic weight to them the same as when Uncle Kingsley let me hold his police revolver. Was like holding the sword of King Arthur in your hands, it was more than heavy metal, it was untamed destiny in that revolver. I couldn't bring myself to point it.

A cigarette pack felt the same way exactly and even though I knew corn silk was a better smoke, a finer and more entertaining smoke, it was not the equal of a cigarette. Same as a slingshot was not the equal of Uncle Kingsley's thirty-eight even though I wanted it to be and thought the world unfair 'cause it wasn't so.

It bothered me for a long time that I had in the field
the best smokes ever and yet I knew I was gonna have
to get up enough courage and think of a believable lie
to tell Mrs. Pierce at the grocery. "They're for my Uncle
Bob" and I knew she knew I didn't have an Uncle Bob.
All the while I was satisfied with corn silk only it weren't
packaged right and Nat King Cole didn't and Bob Hope
didn't and Chester A. Arthur didn't, even though corn
silk was a good fine smoke.

You Shoot it,
You Eat it

We called it "the commandment." Number eleven followed the well-known first ten. Number eleven was by our dad, not by God. As a result we observed the eleventh a lot tighter than the others and knew from this our first moral lesson. If you want a commandment to stick, do unto them what our dad did. He said, "You shoot it, you eat it."

That the 11th commandment was simple proved Dad was either smarter than Moses or else Moses was a lawyer meaning Moses couldn't write simple commandments. Nothing plain like "you shoot it, you eat it." The commandments one to ten have a pattern, they ain't plain, they smell of litigation.

Take ol' number one, "Thou shalt have no other gods before me." Right from the beginning there's a problem and any chance of getting a conviction is remote. Not to mention the difficulty with scale. Commandment number one is outta proportion to the township, the common affairs of folks are summed up by lying, cheating, stealing hub caps, spittin', chewin' and staying up late so what does the first law of Moses say? God is number one. It isn't a commandment but a commercial. Besides, what does no other gods before me mean?

That God doesn't like to stand in line? That God doesn't like to share? Is this very nice?

How about thou shalt not bear false witness? What do you suppose this means? That we shouldn't tell lies about bears? Moses is hiding something, notably a scheme to employ Bible scholars. Same thing happens with speed limits, the sign says 65 mph. So who drives 65 when everybody gets away with 67-68, 70 if wearing Illinois plates? Why doesn't the sign say, "about 65 mph?" We know why, because ever since Moses statutory law has been elastic. A farmer knows he can't build a fence this way, either its barbed wire strung to concert pitch or the cows ain't gonna mind it.

Thou shalt not commit adultery. For a long time I had a hard time figuring out what this one meant and I don't think I was the only kid confused. Moses is real shrewd with this one, I think he is covering his tracks. Talk about protracted legal argument. Not only is it years before the average kid knows what the heck is involved, the point is obscured by the intentional use of an uncertain verb. Commandment says you gotta commit adultery not just do it. Commitment isn't the goal of the average hobbyist, commit is the verb of the professional. Moses is leaving room for the freak storm, the dalliance, the rare chance and statistical aberration. This commandment alone insured the legal profession, a humanity followed by the carrion-scented as long as human beings care to exist.

The commandments are like those white picket fences around some houses, they ain't much good as a fence. Not meant to keep anything out as to augment the architecture. The commandments might have said something about brushing teeth or drinking milk or not smoking in bed or picking the neighbor's asparagus. If the commandments had given sensible advice the world would have been better off, read books, save money, plant trees, chew your food, write to friends and feed the birds. Imagine the wholesale improvement had the commandments taken up housekeeping and personal hygiene. Like taking a bath and keeping your room neat and getting exercise and eating a good breakfast. Moses knew moral edification weren't gonna change anything. Saying folks oughtn't kill and steal and lie is like saying they oughtn't put their head under a cement block. They already know it hurts.

My dad understood the commandments were too much lengthwise measure and not enough thick. They wouldn't support the weight of human travail. The only time the law of Moses got close to the ground was when it said "thou shalt not steal." Even a lawyer couldn't dodge this one without devoted effort. If you want a commandment to work dab-on without saving money for litigation then do like my dad, "you shoot it, you eat it." Attach that model legislation to murder and trespass and you'll get an early improvement to the affairs of Man.

The eleventh commandment came into being when my older brother got a Red Ryder BB gun. I mean a holy cow, genuine, honest to god, everactionwoodstock-bluebarrelrockymountainsightsgoldembossedrapidfire defenderofthefrontierchildrenandwomenfolktriggerha ppy500shot BB gun. The best thing ever made by Man to restore democracy where it is most lacking, namely to farmkids who are about the most oppressed population on the earth except for girls.

Got it on his birthday wrapped in freezer paper; our mother wrapped everything in freezer paper. We knew right off it was a BB gun 'cause it had that... that... weight... that specific soul-scaring gravity only guns have. Nothing else feels the serious caliber of a gun. After he opened it Dad said the eleventh Commandment. Said it once same as God said to Moses. "You shoot it, you eat it."

Boy did that fix things. Here we had a precision BB gun good for off-hand shots at 50 yards and Dad saying "you shoot it you eat it." We didn't have to ask what he meant, we knew, we shoot it we eat it.

So we ate 'em. Gophers, sparrows, chipmunks, grasshoppers. Once I shot a bluebird and ate it. Were the most awful thing I ever done and pulling the feathers off that poor beastie and cooking it and eating it made a bad sin even worse. Dad knew it wasn't enough to confess sin and transgression. People don't improve if they can bury their mistakes. If they have to pull the feathers off their sins and gut them and eat 'em raw or cooked over green wood they won't sin again, at least not without a bad taste in their mouth.

Dad was the same with everything not just BB guns. Hit a cat with the hay mower in the field you ate that cat. Well not exactly ate it but you had to do more than just let it go off and die. If it was hurt bad you killed it all the way, if only a bit hurt you brought it home to fix. Same with killdeer nests, rabbits, fox kits; you bang it you fix it.

When we shot out the mow window with the BB gun we ate it. I mean we had to put new panes in it using the double ladder which was the only one that reached far enough and this while standing on tiptoe with nothing but a knothole to wrap our eyelid around. I'd rather swim the Atlantic Ocean underwater as fix that window again.

Like Pa said, "You shoot it, you eat it."

Awful

The crow is the most antique of animals, it predates the dinosaur, the trilobite and the archangel. God did not make the crow. When God arrived at this unplowed dark, the crow was perched on a limb of drear waiting for the match to touch off the kindling. The crow didn't need making any more than God but was glad for the company.

The crow coulda done without the other animals; not only were they all lower than him, they were less interesting. Fool animals with picky appetites and too much sentiment, upholstery animals excepting the naked chicken as put on airs of being blood-relation to old spark himself and it the most out-of-luck beast you ever wanna see, assuming you could stand to look at it. Damnation if a rock didn't have more raiment, and them all the while carryin' on how they's kin to the original smoke. The crow knew a lie when he saw one, never mind it was a remarkable lie. Mr. Crow took up the hobby of keeping track of that human animal who sometimes took carrion to extremes, even for a crow who appreciates extermination better than most. Which is how come everyplace as thinks it's somewhere has a worry of crows perched in the trees. Like as not speculating on fate and sassing humanity, hoping somebody falls dead soon 'cause it's supper time and they ain't much particular who long as the meal's served on time. Cuisine doesn't matter to a crow any more than it does to a lumberjack long as it's most ways dead.

Had a crow once. Truth is the ownership went the other way around... the crow had me more than I had it. My mama named him, said it was an awful bird on account the standard noise a crow comes equipped with. High-pitched vibration whose oscillation can carry six miles on a quiet evening and simple enough to repeat. Crows aren't given to hyperbole, they do not believe in adjectives except in the rare case, truth requires neither polish or paint. Ain't into rhetoric either and don't much care for style being it too is polish and like as not a distance from the truth. Awful was his name.

I discovered Awful in Widow Soik's field on a snowy evening having spied him from my window in the school bus. Keeping a patch thawed enough to see out kept me busy from the moment I left school till I disembarked. They didn't heat the bus on purpose so to keep farm-kids occupied. Thawing window was a full-time thing; breathing on a spot half an hour to soften the ice, then scrape away a layer of frost with your mitten if you were a weenie or lick it off with your tongue if you weren't. Some kids didn't breathe it soft in the first place and froze their tongues to the window which looked damned odd going down the road. There weren't no trouble-makers on my bus in the winter 'ceptin' some mumbled, as went with the season.

Might as well look through a kaleidoscope and expect to see London as through a bus window but I seen 'em anyhow, back from the road a tangle of crows, probably a raiding party swarming over some hapless appetizer laying prostrate if not quite deceased. Half to escape evening chores, half curious I waded through the snow to discover the injured one. The right wing so very broken it was perpendicular to its opposite member yet the bird struggling to make the night roost, urged on by its kinsmen. A bubbling wound the color of cherry pop suggested vanity was involved, a trait I hadn't thought crows partial to.

I looked at the bird that long minute. Being a farmkid I knew the death business well enough. If a creature is of a mind to croak, its eyes say so even though the rest of it is flapping around. Best to then to leave it for the night and its owl. This crow did not act the least bit inclined to glorifying an owl's innards. As if to second the motion, when I reached down it muttered sourly but came along without fuss. I bundled the crow inside my jacket with its head poking out, having conveniently forgotten about the blood and that I was wearing my school duds. Mama didn't mind blood and cow stink on work clothes but was jealous of school clothes. The crow complained at first about the view, then the room temperature, after that it just hung on as I swam for the town road, the snow melting inside the galoshes I had forgotten to buckle.

Mama was not in agreement with my optimism of saving the crow. "It's wild, you know." Why adults say stupid things like this I don't know. "God didn't intend crows for household pets." Well, I didn't think God intended farmboys for arithmetic neither, but didn't offer the observation.

Mama being the spokesman for God kept us current with the goings-on in heaven. How Mama knew the personal thoughts of God and a majority of the saints I didn't understand and won't have cared to learn. Came with being a witch I suppose, Mama being one. Which explains her intimate knowledge of the celestial parts and her ability to heal. My mama could raise the dead. Did it hundreds of times, seen her do it. Sick puppies, underweight calves, orphaned lambs, kittens fragile as a cobweb. Animals as close to toast as you can get and not lathered over with blackberry jam. From her store of poultices and balms she fussed a paste, a broth of leaves and quack grass, and an animal as had every right obligation to die survived and became prosperous. Meaning it died at a proper time, with the farm account in mind. Mama did for the crow what she had for countless doomed creatures, a splint and a swaddle of bandages. Awful was not about be handled like any emergency room vagrant and said as much. Mama snapped her index finger against his bill and he quit his commentary. After all, he was messing with God's emissary. After which she dismissed me and the now mummified beast to the evening chores for which I was overdue. The crow did not object as I perched him on a pipeline away from the cats who he watched with his dark consuming eyes. I don't know what consuming means when it comes to eyes but it sounds powerful. I wager crows inspect the world with something akin to corporate greed 'cause they ain't the sort to waste emotion on liberal attitudes.

Awful recovered in the next month, soon after the crow took over the management and ownership of the farm. A series of perches was scattered around the house and farm, we came to think of them as bully pulpits. A miscellaneous construct of stick and lath, forming at the top a crude tee-bar. The kitchen had its perch, the milk-house, the barn alley, the living room, one was mounted on the Ford tractor, another on the Allis Chalmers. Everywhere we went Awful came too except the kirk on Sunday morning as could have stood the improvement even more than farm chores.

Awful civilized quick enough, a simple transaction when you think about it. Society isn't railroads or electricity or high-heeled shoes. A person can eat with their hands, smoke old tires and bathe no more than leap year... don't matter to civilization as long as they don't poop indoors. Awful soon learned this rudimentary ingredient to polite company.

According to Mama's great Aunt Hanna who was a witch from way back, when Noah was told to build an ark he had trouble following the instructions, being God wasn't the sort for blueprints. To wit Noah hired a crow to help him figure out the wherewithal of marine construction since Noah hadn't built a ferry boat before, in fact not even a rowboat. Barns and granaries and outhouses but not an ark, not an End-of-the-world Grade-A Apocalypse Raft. Other animals applied for the position of marine engineer and so did the brother-in-law but Noah hired the crow from its competent appearance, exactly the what-for required by a paramilitary cataclysm. When Noah put a timber wrong or misplaced a bulkhead that crow let out a chorus of criticism; in the end Noah had a more or less waterproof boat capable of floating over forty days of damnation, for at this the crow was expert.

The rain began with cats and dogs then turned up the rate to horses and rhinos. Before it was over the rain was coming down in Bengal tigers and tyrannosaurus rex. The animals willing to be saved were herded up according to the instructions in the manual of ruin. The crow felt slighted at this casual dismissal of his extensive relation and petitioned Mister Noah to allow him a few of the choicer cousins. Noah feeling obligated to the crow for his able assistance granted the wish. This why in the worst gales of that forty day cruise a murder of crows in the mast-wood kept counsel with Noah, the other animals not being well schooled in cataclysm. Blessed by their navigation, the ark was kept from hitting reefs and running aground at Newfoundland which is a touch worse than drowning. The crows never once disappointed

Noah even though they didn't have the slightest idea where they were either. Experience had taught crows the premium ingredient for survival during a time of heck is staying cool; crows to this day still preach it. 'Course it's got a Hebrew accent which is to be expected being God was their cousin. Noah and the crows got on swell, civilized birds they did it over open water which weren't hard to find in the circumstance, never mind the pigeons couldn't. This explains why the general category of animals was restricted to a tight interpretation of the two-by-two clause in the Book of Ruin. And why you'll find crows over every decent place on earth, London and Amsterdam, over New York City and Chattanooga, everywhere as is the least bit habitable has crows. 'Cause they're civilized. Which don't explain the pigeon. This how come the crow ain't endangered as the eagle, the condor and the bobolink. 'Cause not only is the crow house-broken, but so very civilized as to not taste good, as any can see is a high grade of genius. Which of course does explain pigeons.

Were God of a mind to admire creation without attracting autograph seekers, he could do worse than go hiking disguised as a crow. Everyone knows you can't see any raw expanse of fate from the vantage of a blue-eyed animal like a badger, any more than a gentile psychiatrist can hope to understand heavy caliber demonology. God could go tramping the universe as a crow and not feel one whit diminished.

Story goes that when it finally quit raining and the wind calmed, Noah sent a crow to look for dry land. How the Book says the crow didn't return so Noah cast out a pigeon who came back with an olive branch. So where you suppose the olive branch came from? The report didn't honestly comprehend crow behavior 'cause a crow as ain't come back has found dry land sure as anything and is setting up a homestead. Bad news been had the crow come back, meaning water water everywhere and the damnation still in effect. By the time Noah hit the coast the crow had a garden planted, olive trees too and the first crop of peas and taters ready for folks who had a bellyful of sea biscuits. Crow knew how to plant taters same as it knew how to build the ark.

Awful ate supper in the farm kitchen with the rest of us, perched next to the red-eyed radio. Sometimes he made more noise than the radio only you could turn the radio off. On the meal's adjournment he took his perch in the living room where he favored Paladin over other choices recognizing the sophistication a black-hat and chess-playing brings to the hero business. At bedtime Awful had a post at the corner of my bed. He'd sleep hunched over, the drapes of his eyes pulled tight. For a wild thing he sure slept hard.

You'd think he'd fall off being asleep but he never did. Was like his feet never did sleep, never relaxed, never let go which is a standard property of the supernatural. In the morning he commenced a chortling sound like a verse from a Buddhist poem, half-supplication, half chuckle, them being the mirthful sort of Buddhists. Awful didn't care for morning same as my dad who was at the milking before dawn; like said, the crow is an advanced civilization. Not the immoral behavior of wrens, cardinals and chickadees who grow impatient when dark is still 18-carat pure. The crow is no early riser, a regular Solomon permitting the owl who is another immoral bird one last survey of the meadow. Rather than force the issue the crow allows the owl his solitary. Not till the sun breaks the horizon was Awful willing to leave his station and if I yet tardy he roused me with a skull-crushing machine-gun burst of awful noise. A sound so caustic at close range I'd rather been shot at by a cannon loaded with scrap nails. Eventually Awful learned the window latch himself and with a deft twist of his beak opened the casement. A natural pick-pocket if ever I knew one, which may or may not have something to do with godliness.

My second story bedroom overlooked the central keep of the farmyard, to one side the granary, opposite the red flank of the barn. At the window ledge Awful composed himself, a strange preparation as if he was dubious about his own ability to fly. I swear he always looked at the ground with a lump in his throat. A sparrow won't do this nor a hawk; neither believe gravity has anything to do with them, which again is why the crow is so darn wise, 'cause it doubts the obvious. Awful stepped off the edge and swooped across the interval to the barn in a silent glide not once flapping his wings. Neatly banking through the barn door to land on the spine of the first cow in the milking alley. The cows learned to cope with Awful's sudden appearance after numerous attempts to pull their heads off. Eventually they came to appreciate Awful as a resident chiropractor tending their backbones, such was their ecstasy their tails stood straight up. During humid summers as favor cattle flies, Awful picked the grubs beneath their skin; the cows got shuck of a terrible itch and Awful had lunch.

The crow went to every chore with us, his favorite was a toss-up between haying and spreading manure. At haying the sickle bar sometimes wounded juvenile birds and broke up nests. Clamped to the cultivator lever, Awful watched the ground, seeing something interesting he'd tilt off his perch, swing down and swallow with the efficiency of a vacuum cleaner the still-convulsing victim.

Manuring the fields was a dangerous job, the missiles you see and the ones you don't. Sodden, brown missiles, missiles the size of rag rugs flung in the air by the beaters. Awful rode the shoulder of the tractor driver not trusting the aim of beaters as sometimes pitched shrapnel in every direction. From time to time he'd swirl up to investigate a residue neglected by the digestive tract of the last owner. His favorite being the still-warm kernels of corn, a taste so exquisite his eyes rolled back same as you see in patrons of a french restaurant.

When a thing died on the farm Awful was the first to attend the funeral. It bothered me at first to watch him pluck the eyes of dead cats and calves; wasn't the least bit surgical, more like tug-o-war till the rope broke. Awful perceived no insult in death, instead it was the most orderly principle at work in creation, without which the whole shebang fly apart, life rendered utterly meaningless because nothing ever croaked. According to the crow testament life, it's the result of death doing its honest transaction.

Heroism wasn't one of Awful's traits. At the first sight of anything questionable or bigger than himself he'd retreat until it either bit off someone else or proved benign. Put alone in a dark room, he'd bleat like a lost lamb until someone came to share the dark. But give him company and a solid perch and he'd ride to war out-gunned, out-numbered, out-smarted. He particularly liked the Allis Chalmers WD in fourth gear, the throttle pulled to the bottom. Sixteen miles per hour full tilt, Awful clamped on the cultivator lever, wings out, beak leaning into the wind. God, I liked the pose. They shoulda done a coin after him.

A neighbor shot Awful by mistake. Thought he was a crow. I thought some about mistaking my neighbor for a thief.

Boxelders

I started climbing trees shortly after learning to walk, followed immediately by treehouses. Later I was weaned and introduced to solid food. If anthropologists really want to learn the behavior of early humanoids, they'll quit wasting time on primates and study farmkids.

When I was a child, trees were the place. Despite my tender age, I conducted an analysis of the world's premium predators and found by my survey few of them pursued the main course into the branches.

All my imaginary monsters and hypothetical dragons were earthbound, excepting, as reported previously, the artful Clyde hawk with its 90-foot wing span as could nip a kid off a barn roof after dark, be the kid so foolish to remain on the roof after dark, without a BB gun. Happily, this economy-size gastronome was offended by boxelder trees. The very smell of boxelders did something to its olfactory sense and it hied from any of that vegetation.

As is the luck of farmsteads, I was surrounded and fortressed by boxelders. The tree disdained by architects, denounced by horticulturists, dynamited by developers, and reviled by everyone with an educated sensitivity, held the farmstead in its embrace. It hugged every building and outhouse. The appearance from a distance was of a gleeful green swaddle in whose midst somewhere was a farm.

Never was a boxelder anywhere as grew straight. Maple, oak, walnut, hickory, pine, ash, birch go on to honest timber. Not boxelder. From the outset this tree is a cripple. It comes out of the ground as a pleasant sort of green shoot and immediately takes detour. Long before other trees start their lateral branching, the boxelder is already at it. My mama would point at boxelders and warn that is what would happen if I smoked cigarettes. That I'd grow up all crooked and humpback and prone to break at every wind storm. I took up whittling.

I had of course noted the miscalculation in my mother's sermon. While the boxelder is a convalescent looking tree, always recovering from another severed limb, it was remarkably unkillable. A crack the size of Vermont smack down the middle of any other kind of tree will kill it in due order. Not the boxelder.

Somehow boxelders were aware of the low opinion the human race had of their species and contrived a strategem to defeat the prejudice. It took root under every eave of every shed, every garage, ice house, outhouse, pig keep, smoke house, woodchance on the farm. Unnoticed, it grew to middle age and by the time the farmer decided to extract the weed, it had grown onto the building and could not be discharged without extracting the majority of the building as well. Its roots slithered under foundations, wormed under footing and post. To have out any one tree was to imperil every building on the place, including the septic tank; the tree could not be moved.

The farm of my youth was surrounded by boxelders. If the fields lay flat and servile with fence rows neatly stitched, so the township appeared the coverlet of an enormous bed, the one interference was the boxelder, whose covert shielded the stead, the barnyard and front porch from what appeared to be contagious fields. The farmhouse was cooler in summer, and the cows more content, through the benefit of that good for nothing weed.

Out behind the car garage, between the ice house and the machine shed stood a coven of boxelders. Six massive trees, each with a beam equal to a frigate, and every one of them equipped with more mast than a tea clipper. Their limbs were horrendously tangled, the trunk gut-shot and crippled, not a single board foot of these trees went plumb in three directions at once. The wood of them could not be burned in the stove without issuing the same heart-wrenching burble as when a farmer tries to drown kittens. The only part that burned was the windfalls, these my grandmother collected every Saturday morning to stoke her kitchen range.

Superior intelligence in a tree is a remarkable thing. Every behavior and trait of the boxelder indicated intelligence of the sublime type… the sort of calculation found in a chess master. The tree could not be checkmated, always playing to a draw whether to the farmstead or with propriety.

As I was saying, there were on the farm these broken back boxelders who, despite every infirmity, continued to thrive. The trunks of these wounded gargoyles swung so low to the ground, the merest infant could get a foothold, then step by step soar to the celestial region. By merely following the trunk the child became airborne, every day another limb higher, the hand a little stronger, the balance better. Mothers, if they have any faith in divine Nature, learned early to avert their gaze and leave the child to its fate, particularly were it a farmkid.

Soon the kid is astride a high branch in that green heaven, aware of the divine intercession of seeing all things from an advantage. Then it was on to a higher tree, a tree the kid must hug with arms and legs and teeth to climb. Or build a ladder from scrap lumber and, once a length of haymow rope is installed, burn the ladder. The only way to the tree's rare place was by this one avenue alone, forbidding the weak and the frightened from entering. In most cases this meant girls, little brothers and mothers.

As I remember childhood, there was once a fortification where a kid was safe. They knew where you had gone but they couldn't follow, perhaps it was that they chose not to. To let the child have his tree and the tree its child, for there are things only the high place can teach. You can see on farmers the mark of those tutored by trees. Who sat on the bough with the Maker and watched the world. A witness to things otherwise concealed; the eye, tree-taught, is more seeing than tiger and eagle. Known is every leaf and its fall, every stone and seed, every shadow and burrow. And too, the horizon's curve into the night with a roundness the land below can't know.

A hundred thousand years it was, give or take, before Copernicus and Galileo, the tree borne knew of creation's roundness. Knew it because they had been to the tree and climbed beyond what earth knew. Knew what only archangels had before. This, for those who hang on trees.

What is a FarmKid?

What is a farmkid and where do they come from? Are they born the same as other children and merely tannic stained by a country place till they are of that separate hue? Neither black or brown or white or freckled but some other defining color? What color is a farmkid? An earth tone surely. Something in pasture green, barn red and cow-yard brown, a hue as pale as winter blizzard, yellow as autumn corn; this is the color of a farmkid.

Farmkids are not entirely human, you can see this if you look close. They angle out where they ought not. They will not take a polish. They are out of round and in places dirt clings secretly. They will if unattended go wading in a mud puddle, sidewalks do not appeal. Well they might grow up to be lawyers and doctors and CEOs, nurses, teachers, ministers, opera stars but out back, down deep, where the village can't see, they are yet and always farmkids.

So where do they come from? Farmkids? We must go back to Genesis to find where farmkids began. When the Great Cumulus as made things like dirt and amino acids and did separate naked man from the water buffalo and the English sparrow, it was in between the jackrabbit and the antelope the Maker did fashion farmkids. Using the same mold as for the bear cub, but without the fur and fewer spots, these were farmkids, human but only sorta.

How can you tell a farmkid from the other kind? Take a window, mount it in the wall of a classroom and the farmkid will tend it, never mind the rest of the class is with Admiral Byrd at the North Pole, the farmkid will reach always for the nearer earth. When this child grows up and has a career in microbiology, the lack of windows will trouble them, a branch with a sparrow is too much to bear.

You can observe, if you wish, farmkids trying to escape, driving north on a miserable, cold weekend to vacation at a cabin without plumbing or central air. See them with that longing look, staring out their car windows as they glide up the Interstate, remembering their father's farm, grandfather's, Uncle Fred's. How they used to, as a kid, spend the summer there; it had an apple tree from where they learned to fly, at least it seemed then like flight. A haymow, too, that pickle patch they learned to hate and its hoe handle, the day as never stopped. There was a stream, paltry little thing, it less gurgled than hiccuped, in it they quenched the fevered day, lay in the shade and watched stars form and darkness come, deeper than they ever thought.

Maybe it is the potato patch remembered, the new calf, the dusty chicken coop, the summer of hay, the humid nights, the irrigation pipe; nobody warned them then they could never let go. Despite a PhD, who really ought know better, and their job pays so well, benefits besides; the farm teases them yet. I have seen them going by on the road looking out of their windows, attached yet by unseen umbilical. Some hunt and imagine they are back, some collect quilts and jugs and Shaker furniture. They dream of a place some day, a house on the end of a lane, a

dog under the porch, wood shed, clothesline. They know
it is an impossible vision, that white fenced pasture, the
barn on the horizon, the plain square house. Scary when
you really think about it, no amenities, no satellite dish, no
computer, no built-in dishwasher, the floor in the kitchen
is linoleum for cripes sake. There's a chicken block and a
drowning pail and you don't even want to see where the
sauerkraut came from. This what makes them farmkids
yet, they know the secret, terrible as it is. Behind it all,
behind the automatic, behind touch pad and the mouse,
behind the precooked, pre-fabbed, perma-press is an
awful truth, a horrible truth. The truth is, for farmkids it
doesn't matter. None of it matters; whatever civilization
thinks it is or where it is going doesn't matter; how ever
much it is polished up and smoothed over. They know
this because they once were something else, someplace
else, they were farmkids. Where what matters is the
sparrow, the cows, and that green place out the window
even if it is a pickle patch.